A COMPLETE MATHS PROGRA
FOR PRIMARY SCHOOLS

Planet Maths

5th Class

Satellite Activity Book

Elaine Burke

FOLENS

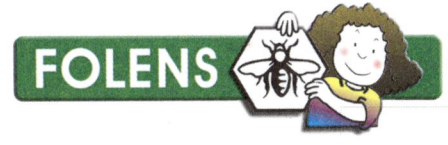

Author: Elaine Burke
Editor: Sarah Deegan and Claire Rourke
Design: Marian Purcell
Layout: Marian Purcell
Illustrators: James Walmesley and Kerry Ingham (GCI)
Photographs: Thinkstock

ISBN: 978-1-84741-788-6

© Folens Publishers, 2011

First published in 2011 by: Folens Publishers,
Hibernian Industrial Estate, Greenhills Road, Tallaght, Dublin 24.

The paper used in this book is sourced from managed forests.

Folens books are protected by international copyright laws. All rights reserved. The copyright of all materials in this book, except where otherwise stated, remains the property of the author(s). No part of this publication may be reproduced, stored in a retrieval system or transmitted in any form or by any means (stencilling, photocopying, etc.) for whatever purpose, even purely educational, without the prior written permission of the publisher. The publisher reserves the right to change, without notice, at any time the specification of this product. The publisher has made every effort to contact copyright holders but if any have been overlooked we will be pleased to make any necessary arrangements. To the best of the publisher's knowledge, information in this book was correct at the time of going to press. No responsibility can be accepted for any errors.

Introduction for Parents and Teachers

Planet Maths is a series of Maths textbooks, activity books and corresponding teacher's manuals for Junior Infants to 6th Class. It is in line with the Revised Primary Curriculum and has been written by primary school teachers. Curriculum Strands, Strand Units and Objectives are detailed throughout. Blue teaching boxes introduce new concepts as they arise.

Planet Maths has been designed to provide students with challenging activities and enjoyable mathematical experiences to help them become confident mathematicians. Pupils using **Planet Maths** will experience mathematical learning through the following approach:

- Learning the new maths skills associated with a topic with the aid of explanation boxes and/or worked examples that introduce each new concept or operation;
- Practising and reinforcing new skills through drills and repetition, while also providing as much variety and stimulation as possible;
- Exploring and applying their skills in 'real life' contexts and situations that are relevant, fun and stimulating to young minds.

'Real life' themed maths features

There are seven two-page 'real life' themed maths features spread throughout the 3rd to 6th Class textbooks. They are **designed to bring Maths to life**, making it more engaging for students by enabling them to use their skills in contexts that are **refreshing**, **relevant** and **interesting** to them. Each 'real life' feature uses the skills and knowledge that pupils have acquired in the preceding units.

Warm-Up Activities

A warm-up activity appears at the beginning of every new topic along with the instruction, 'Listen to your teacher'. These game-like activities open each unit of the senior textbooks and are led by the teacher with directions from the accompanying teacher's manual. Because they are conducted at the start of each unit, these activities provide a **mental warm-up** for students, preparing them to learn by focusing their attention on the teacher. Warm-up activities are based on the **concepts** and **operations** relevant to the topic.

Pair and Group Work

The series recognises the value of collaborative learning and **ample opportunities** are provided throughout the textbooks for both pair work and group work. Maths puzzles suited to pairs, straightforward group activities and oral activities such as 'pretend you are the teacher' are used in the series.

Differentiation

To promote ease of differentiation, a **red line** appears beside a selection of problems and sums in the 3rd to 6th Class textbooks that could prove more challenging for many pupils. Additionally, the 3rd to 6th Class textbooks contain **Challenge Yourself** problems designed to provide early finishers with extra stimulus and reward, and to assist with differentiation.

Self-Assessment

Self-assessment is strong feature of the series. Pupils are encouraged to rate their own performance and understanding of a topic through the use of a **traffic light system** at the end of every page in each topic. Students can assess their performance at the end – red for difficultly, amber for improvement and green for full understanding.

Check Up Activities

Each topic unit concludes with a page of concise check up activities designed to reinforce learning. Check ups include **oral, operational, problem-solving** and **shared activities** based on the topic at hand. Oral activities reinforce **communicating and expressing as a mathematical skill**, and vocabulary-based exercises assess the pupil's understanding of the mathematical language used in the unit.

Mental Maths

Seven dedicated Mental Maths units are placed strategically throughout the 3rd to 6th Class textbooks, with each one including a **Multiple Choice** component. Each section in Mental Maths contains a **score box for pupils to rate their performance**. This will encourage them to collaborate in their own progress and to recognise areas where more effort and assistance is needed.

The Teacher's Manual accompanying this textbook includes:

- A guide providing comprehensive suggestions on how to make the best use of this series.
- Oral and mental maths activity suggestions.
- Maths language relevant to each topic.
- Suggestions for using concrete materials and manipulatives.
- Photocopiable activities for differentiation and extension exercises.
- Photocopiable templates for practice and repetition of fundamental concepts.
- Answers.
- Assessment sheets.
- Individual student profile sheets.
- Class record sheets.

The activity books in the series contain supplementary and differentiation activities. Interactive activities for this series can also be found at: www.folensonline.ie.

Contents

Topic		Page
1.	Place Value	5
2.	Operations	8
3.	Data 1	11
4.	Multiplication 1	14
5.	2D Shapes	17
6.	Division 1	20
7.	Fractions 1	23
8.	Fractions 2	26
9.	Lines and Angles	29
10.	Decimals	32
11.	Problem Solving	35
12.	Number Theory	38
13.	Multiplication 2	41
14.	Length	44
15.	Division of Decimals	47
16.	Time	50
17.	Percentages 1	53
18.	Money	56
19.	Percentages 2	59
20.	Area	62
21.	Directed Numbers	65
22.	The Circle	68
23.	Rules and Properties	71
24.	Weight	74
25.	Number Sentences	77
26.	3D Shapes	80
27.	Data 2	83
28.	Capacity	86
29.	Chance	89
	Revision	92

TOPIC 1 Place Value

A. Warm Up!

In your copy, show each of the following numbers on a notation board.

1. 348
2. 982
3. 1,207
4. 10,498
5. 29,487
6. 34,673
7. 19,276
8. 82,846
9. 69,387
10. 50,832

B. In your mathematical opinion

1. Estimate and then count how many numbers between 1,000 and 10,000 have a zero in them.   estimate: _____   count: _____
2. How many numbers between 1,000 and 10,000 have two zeros in them? _____
3. How many numbers between 1,000 and 10,000 have three zeros in them? _____

C. Calculate!

1. Round each of these numbers to the nearest 10.

    (a) 62 _____   (b) 275 _____   (c) 594 _____
    (d) 1,273 _____   (e) 5,491 _____   (f) 10,751 _____
    (g) 23,656 _____   (h) 34,623 _____   (i) 73,869 _____   (j) 97,451 _____

2. Round each of the following numbers to the nearest 100.

    (a) 78 _____   (b) 174 _____   (c) 216 _____   (d) 1,288 _____   (e) 8,439 _____
    (f) 18,958 _____   (g) 29,609 _____   (h) 39,178 _____   (i) 77,832 _____   (j) 83,921 _____

3. Round each of the following numbers to the nearest 1,000.

    (a) 1,297 _____   (b) 2,399 _____   (c) 4,879 _____   (d) 7,952 _____   (e) 9,088 _____
    (f) 18,548 _____   (g) 38,752 _____   (h) 54,545 _____   (i) 40,523 _____   (j) 75,101 _____

D. Puzzle

| 4 | 8 | 5 | 3 | 9 |

1. How many different 5-digit number can you make from these numerals? _____
2. What is the greatest 5-digit number and smallest and 5-digit number that can be made?
   greatest: _____   smallest: _____
3. What number can you make that is closest to 60,000? _____
4. What number can you make that is closest to 45,000? _____

E. Real-life maths

Mike is a teller in a bank.

1. In your copy, help Mike to fill in the missing information on each bank draft.

(a)
BANK NAME
DATE: 02 / 04 / 16
PAY: 11,283.94
TO THE ORDER OF: _____ EURO
SIGNED: M. Byrne
01990 76589 41425 3219 00 23650

(b)
BANK NAME
DATE: 05 / 04 / 16
PAY: _____
TO THE ORDER OF: Twenty-one thousand, four hundred and sixty-nine euro and 85c
SIGNED: J. McCormack
01990 76589 41425 3219 00 23650

(c)
BANK NAME
DATE: 06 / 04 / 16
PAY: 30,004.16
TO THE ORDER OF: _____
SIGNED: S. Dunne
01990 76589 41425 3219 00 23650

2. What is the least number of notes and coins that Mike will use to cash these cheques for his customers? He can use €500, €200, €100, €50, €20, €10 and €5 notes and €2, €1, 50c 20c, 10c, 5c, 2c and 1c coins.
   (a) _____   (b) _____
   (c) _____   (d) _____

F. True or false?

1. The value of the 5 in 589 is five hundreds. ☐ true ☐ false
2. The value of the 5 in 2,854 is five units. ☐ true ☐ false
3. The value of the 4 in 41,859 is four thousands. ☐ true ☐ false
4. The value of the 3 in 63,878 is three ten thousands. ☐ true ☐ false
5. There are two thousands in 2,985. ☐ true ☐ false
6. There are one hundred and ninety-eight 10s in 1,984. ☐ true ☐ false
7. There are twelve ten thousands in 12,958. ☐ true ☐ false
8. There are four hundred and fifty-seven units in 457. ☐ true ☐ false
9. There are thirty-eight thousands in 38,683. ☐ true ☐ false

Test yourself!

1. What is 48,731 in expanded form?
   - ☐ 40,000 + 7000 + 800 + 30 + 1
   - ☐ 80,000 + 4000 + 700 + 30 + 1
   - ☐ 30 + 700 + 40,000 + 8,000 + 1
   - ☐ 70,000 + 400 + 8000 + 30 + 1

2. What is the value of the underlined digits in words? <u>5</u>7,583
   - ☐ five thousand, seven hundred
   - ☐ fifty thousand, seven hundred
   - ☐ fifty-seven hundred
   - ☐ fifty-seven thousand

3. What is the value of the underlined digits in numbers? 6<u>4,5</u>98
   - ☐ 45,000
   - ☐ 45
   - ☐ 4,500
   - ☐ 450

4. Round 39,857 to the nearest 10.
   - ☐ 39,860
   - ☐ 40,000
   - ☐ 39,900
   - ☐ 39,000

5. Round 71,867 to the nearest 10.
   - ☐ 71,860
   - ☐ 71,570
   - ☐ 72,000
   - ☐ 71,870

6. Round 85,015 to the nearest 100.
   - ☐ 85,000
   - ☐ 85,000
   - ☐ 85,500
   - ☐ 85,020

7. What is 49,087 in words?
   - ☐ Forty-nine thousand and seventy-eight
   - ☐ Ninety-four thousand and eighty-seven
   - ☐ Forty-nine thousand, eight hundred and seven
   - ☐ Forty-nine thousand and eighty-seven

8. How many 10,000s in 98,735?
   - ☐ 98
   - ☐ 9
   - ☐ 9·8
   - ☐ none

9. How many 1,000s in 56,788
   - ☐ 5
   - ☐ 56
   - ☐ 567
   - ☐ none

rough work

Planet Maths Activity Book • 5th Class

TOPIC 2 Operations

A. Warm up!

Try these in your head.

1. 27 + 34 = _____
2. 1068 − 144 = _____
3. 11,000 − 2,250 = _____
4. 101 + 99 = _____
5. 2,904 − 1,672 = _____
6. 24,500 + 12,900 = _____
7. 394 − 68 = _____
8. 10,000 + 9,461 = _____
9. 55,750 − 46,850 = _____

B. Estimate

1. How many people attended the last World Cup final? _____
2. How many years does 50,000 days make? _____
3. How long would it take you to run 10,000 metres? _____

C. Calculate

1. (a) 14,263
   + 145

   (b) 34,369
   − 2,492

   (c) 11,295
   + 44,286

   (d) 11 + 14,355 + 1,812 = _____
   (e) 28,662 + 45 + 811 = _____
   (f) 19,224 − 89 = _____
   (g) 34,472 − 1,049 = _____

2. (a) Find the sum of 122, 4, 768 and 13,249. _____
   (b) Find the sum of 7, 73, 711 and 26. _____
   (c) From the sum of 8,269 and 19,410 subtract 848 _____
   (d) What is the difference between 24,864 and 11,109? _____
   (e) What is the difference between 64,291 and 33,887? _____

8 Planet Maths Activity Book • 5th Class   Based on Planet Maths 5 pages 14, 15, 16, 17 and 18

D. True or false?

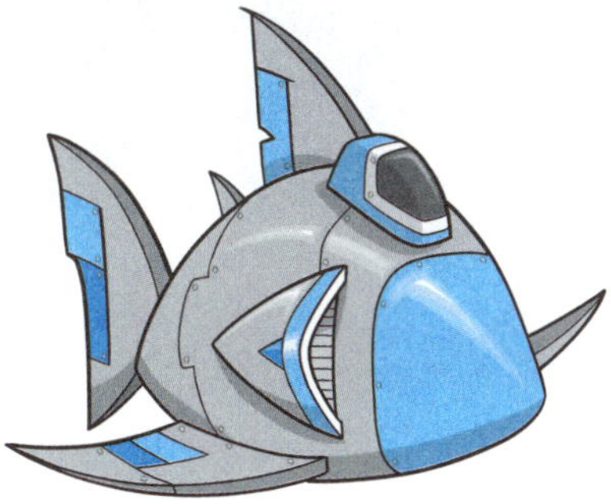

1. 24 less than 1,000 is 924.   □ true □ false
2. 2,500 more than 10,000 is 22,500.   □ true □ false
3. 8,022 is 14,687 less than 22,709.   □ true □ false
4. 19,214 is 4,025 more than 15,189.   □ true □ false
5. 17,241 is 9,847 greater than 7,394.   □ true □ false
6. 64,298 is 19,753 greater than 44,545.   □ true □ false

E. Real-life maths

Lena River:	4,400km	Yellow River:	5,464km
Mississippi-Missouri:	6,275km	Ob-Irtysh:	5,410km
Amazon:	6,400km	Chang Jiang:	6,300km
Congo:	4,700km	Amur-Argun:	4,444km
Yenisei-Angara-Selenga:	5,539km	Nile:	6,650km

1. In your copy, write these rivers in order, starting with the longest.
2. What is the difference between the lengths of the Nile and the Amazon? _____
3. What is the sum of the lengths of the following: Lena, Yellow and Chang Jiang? _____
4. The difference between the lengths of the Amur-Argun and the _____ is 44km.
5. The sum of the lengths of the Mississippi-Missouri and the _____ is 11,685km.
6. Which river is 764km longer than the Congo? _____
7. Which river is 1,956km shorter than the Amazon? _____

F. World puzzles

1. **28,224** people attended a football match on Sunday. The following Sunday **5,683** fewer people attended a match. How many people were at the second match? _____
2. **68,223** copies of *The Evening Times* were sold in September. In October **11,772** more copies were sold. How many copies were sold in October? _____ 
3. **30,098** people attended a rock concert. **18,219** were men. How many women attended the concert? _____

Test yourself!

1. What do you do to find the sum of two numbers?
   - ☐ add
   - ☐ subtract
   - ☐ multiply
   - ☐ divide

2. A reasonable estimate for 12,409 + 38,688 is:
   - ☐ 55,000
   - ☐ 51,000
   - ☐ 48,000
   - ☐ 52,000

3. The difference between 18 and 200 is:
   - ☐ 218
   - ☐ 3,600
   - ☐ 1,122
   - ☐ 182

4. The difference between 64,209 and 46 is:
   - ☐ 18,209
   - ☐ 64,255
   - ☐ 59,409
   - ☐ 64,163

5. What do you do to find the difference between two numbers?
   - ☐ add
   - ☐ subtract
   - ☐ multiply
   - ☐ divide

6. The sum of 8, 26,224, 87 and 4,200 is:
   - ☐ 39,294
   - ☐ 30,519
   - ☐ 39,204
   - ☐ 21,929

7. A supermarket sold 17,211 cans of cola in December, 14,869 in January and 15,008 in February. Altogether it sold:
   - ☐ 50,000
   - ☐ 47,000
   - ☐ 47,088
   - ☐ 74,088

8. To the nearest 100, the number 11,050 is:
   - ☐ 11,000
   - ☐ 11,100
   - ☐ 10,900
   - ☐ 11,200

9. To the nearest 1,000, the number 14,450 is:
   - ☐ 14,400
   - ☐ 14,000
   - ☐ 14,500
   - ☐ 15,000

10. 58,094 tickets were printed for a raffle. After the raffle had been held, there were 19,565 tickets left over. How many tickets were sold?
    - ☐ 38,529
    - ☐ 77,659
    - ☐ 35,829
    - ☐ 39,825

rough work

TOPIC 3: Data 1

A. Warm up!

What type of graph is each of the following?

1. 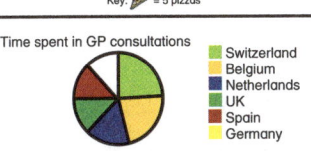 _____

2. 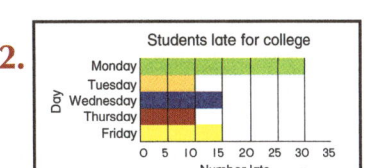 _____

3. 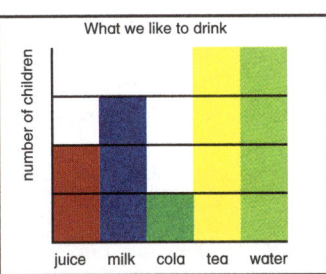 _____

4. 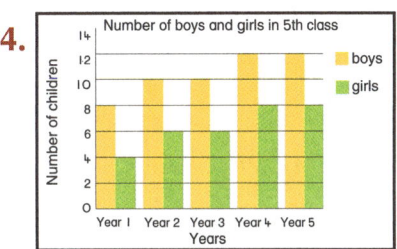 _____

5. 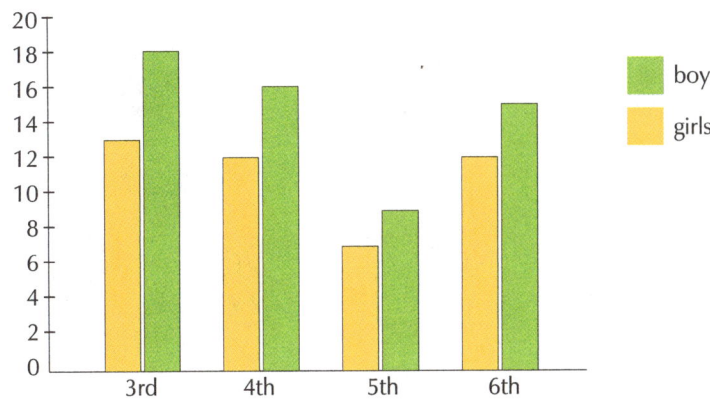 _____

6.
Subject	Tally
Mathematics	＃＃＃ ＃＃＃
Science	＃＃＃ /
Social Studies	＃＃＃ //
Phys. Ed	＃＃＃ ＃＃＃ ///
English	＃＃＃ //

_____

B. Calculate!

This multiple bar chart shows the number of boys and girls in Knockfield National School.

1. How many boys go to Knockfield National School? _____
2. How many children go to Knockfield National School? _____
3. Which class has twelve more girls than boys? _____
4. What is the average number of girls in each class? _____
5. What is the average number of children in each class? _____

Based on Planet Maths 5 pages 19, 20, 21, 22 and 23

D. True or false?

This table show how five teams finished in a soccer league.
A win = 3 points. A draw = 1 point. A loss = 0 points.

Team	played	won	drew	lost	for	against	points
Green Shamrocks	15	9	3	3	24	8	30
Red Dragons	15	8	3	4	21	10	27
Blue Tigers	15	7	4	4	25	12	25
Yellow Birds	15	6	4	5	20	12	22
Black Badgers	15	5	2	8	15	14	17

1. Green Shamrocks scored the most goals. ☐ true ☐ false
2. Blue Tigers had the biggest goal difference (between **for** and **against**). ☐ true ☐ false
3. The Red Dragons has twice as many points as Black Badgers. ☐ true ☐ false
4. The average number of goals scored was 22. ☐ true ☐ false
5. Most of the matches played ended in a draw. ☐ true ☐ false

E. Real-life maths

In your copy. This tally sheet shows the number of hours spent on each subject during two weeks in Oakfield National School.

1. Draw a multiple bar chart to show the information recorded on the tally sheet.

	week 1	won
Maths	𝍬 𝍬 𝍬	𝍬 𝍬 𝍬 I
History	IIII	𝍬
Irish	𝍬 𝍬 III	𝍬 𝍬 IIII
English	𝍬 𝍬 𝍬	𝍬 𝍬 𝍬 𝍬
SPHE	𝍬 I	III
Art	II	I
PE	I	II

2. Write five questions and answers based on the data shown in your multiple bar chart.

Test yourself!

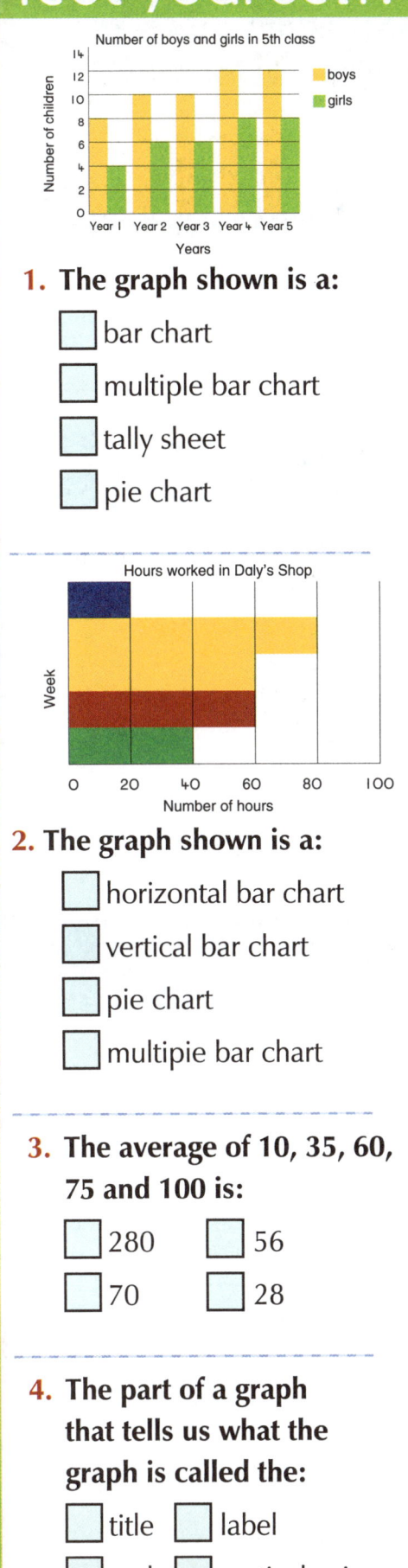

1. The graph shown is a:
   - [ ] bar chart
   - [ ] multiple bar chart
   - [ ] tally sheet
   - [ ] pie chart

2. The graph shown is a:
   - [ ] horizontal bar chart
   - [ ] vertical bar chart
   - [ ] pie chart
   - [ ] multipie bar chart

3. The average of 10, 35, 60, 75 and 100 is:
   - [ ] 280
   - [ ] 56
   - [ ] 70
   - [ ] 28

4. The part of a graph that tells us what the graph is called the:
   - [ ] title
   - [ ] label
   - [ ] scale
   - [ ] vertical axis

5. The part of a graph that tells us what an axis is recording is called the:
   - [ ] title
   - [ ] vertical axis
   - [ ] scale
   - [ ] label

6. This table shows the number of children who were absent from school. How many children, on average, were absent each day during the week?

Monday	7
Tuesday	13
Wednesday	8
Thursday	6
Friday	6

   - [ ] 4
   - [ ] 6
   - [ ] 7
   - [ ] 8

7. This table shows some children's favourite colours. Each child had one vote. How many children were surveyed?

blue	11
pink	4
red	4
black	2
green	9
purple	6

   - [ ] 30
   - [ ] 32
   - [ ] 36
   - [ ] 34

Planet Maths Activity Book • 5th Class

TOPIC 4 Multiplication 1

A. Warm up!

1. Multiply each number by 8:   (a) 4 ___   (b) 6 ___   (c) 12 ___   (d) 18 ___   (e) 20 ___
2. Multiply each number by 10: (a) 8 ___   (b) 14 ___ (c) 22 ___   (d) 240 ___ (e) 580 ___
3. Multiply each number by 100: (a) 3 ___   (b) 11 ___ (c) 32 ___   (d) 110 ___ (e) 201 ___

B. In your mathematical opinion

It takes 2 minutes to brush teeth. If most people brush their teeth twice a day, estimate the following.

1. How much time you spend brushing your teeth in 1 week? _____
2. How much time you spend brushing your teeth in 1 year? _____
3. How much time you spend brushing your teeth over 10 years? _____
4. How much time you spend brushing your teeth over the course of your life?
   (Life expectancy in Ireland is 80 years old.) _____

C. Calculate!

1. (a) 1,468 × 26 = _____   (b) 2,368 × 36 = _____   (c) 1,174 × 25 = _____
   (d) 1·6 × 18 = _____   (e) 2·8 × 14 = _____   (f) 9·4 × 27 = _____
   (g) 3·62 × 29 = _____   (h) 7·71 × 39 = _____   (i) 8·45 × 45 = _____

2. Round each of the following to the nearest whole number.

   (a) 0·8 _____   (b) 1·3 _____   (c) 7·7 _____   (d) 10·5 _____
   (e) 14·77 _____   (f) 25·44 _____   (g) 46·09 _____   (h) 110·84 _____
   (i) $4\frac{1}{2}$ _____   (j) $9\frac{1}{5}$ _____   (k) $11\frac{3}{5}$ _____   (l) $21\frac{9}{10}$ _____

3. Estimate the answers to each of the following.

   (a) 1·87 × 5 = ___   (b) 12·02 × 12 = ___   (c) 202·36 × 12 = ___
   (d) 124·5 × 16 = ___   (e) 426·7 × 22 = ___   (f) 626·14 × 25 = ___

D. Operations

Do you add, subtract, multiply or divide the numbers to find the answers?

1. How many times is 14 contained in 23·8? _____
2. How much bigger is 41·4 than 18? _____
3. What is the difference between 12·64 and 1·12? _____
4. What is the sum of 8, 4·61 and 2·3? _____
5. 20 − ___ = 3·49 _____
6. An athlete can run a kilometre in 3·5 minutes.
   How long will it take him to run 26km? _____
7. Philip thought of the number 6·89. Jean thought of a number seven hundredths smaller than that. What number did Jean think of? _____

E. Real-life maths

	Telemobile	Didphone	Ring out	Dialaphone
off peak 8pm – 8am	11·31c per min	8·79c per min	12·04c per min	10·92c per min
peak 8pm– 8am	15·76c per min	22·42c per min	14·69c per min	16·14c per min

This table shows the cost per minute of making a phone call for each of the four mobile network providers.

1. Which tariff should Peter select if he spends on average 200 minutes talking during peak time and 170 minutes talking during off peak time each month? _____
2. What is the difference per month between the most expensive and the cheapest tariffs? _____

F. Word puzzles

1. By how much is the **6** in **26·15** greater than the 6 in **1·56**? _____
2. From the sum of **13·39** and **1·6** take **4·86**. _____
3. A burger cost **€3·50** and a bag of chips cost **€1·70**. How much did four burgers and six bags of chips cost? _____
4. Christina can walk **0·75km** in **10** minutes. How long will it take her to walk 3km? _____
5. A rubber is made in a factory for **€0·02**. In the shop it is 20 times more expensive. How much would you expect to pay for a rubber in the shop? _____

Test yourself!

1. The number that is 35 times bigger than 14 is:
   - ☐ 21
   - ☐ 49
   - ☐ 490
   - ☐ 175

2. What must be added to 11·75 to make 11·86?
   - ☐ 1·11
   - ☐ 0·011
   - ☐ 0·11
   - ☐ 1·01

3. 1,504 × 26 =
   - ☐ 1,530
   - ☐ 12,032
   - ☐ 31,409
   - ☐ 39,104

4. 1·68 to the nearest whole number is:
   - ☐ 2
   - ☐ 1
   - ☐ 1·7
   - ☐ 1·6

5. 13·69 to the nearest whole number is:
   - ☐ 13
   - ☐ 14
   - ☐ 13·7
   - ☐ 13·6

6. A can of soft drink costs €0·82. How much for 32 cans?
   - ☐ €2·62
   - ☐ €262·40
   - ☐ €26·24
   - ☐ €32·82

7. A running track is 3·23km long. An athlete ran 15 laps. How far did she run?
   - ☐ 484·5km
   - ☐ 4,845km
   - ☐ 4·84km
   - ☐ 48·45km

8. A bucket can hold 1·2 litres. An oil tank can hold one thousand times that amount. How many litres can the oil tank hold?
   - ☐ 120 litres
   - ☐ 1,200 litres
   - ☐ 12,000 litres
   - ☐ 12 litres

9. If €1 is $1·27, €100 is:
   - ☐ $12·70
   - ☐ $127
   - ☐ $1,270
   - ☐ $12,700

10. If €1 is 17·46 yen, €50:
    - ☐ 873 yen
    - ☐ 87·3 yen
    - ☐ 8,730 yen
    - ☐ 87,300 yen

rough work

TOPIC 5 — 2D Shapes

A. Warm-up!

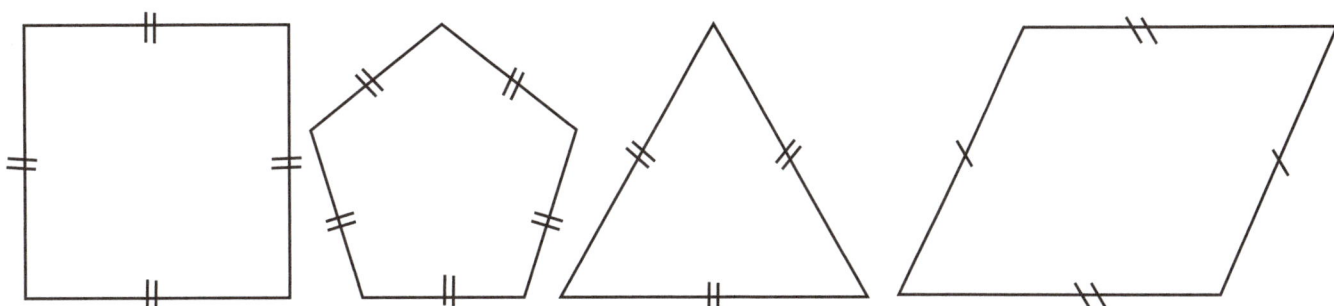

1. Compare and contrast the square and the equilateral triangle. How are they similar? How are they different?

   _____
   _____

2. Compare and contrast the pentagon and the parallelogram. How are they similar? How are they different?

   _____
   _____

B. Calculate!

1. Write the name of each of these shapes.

   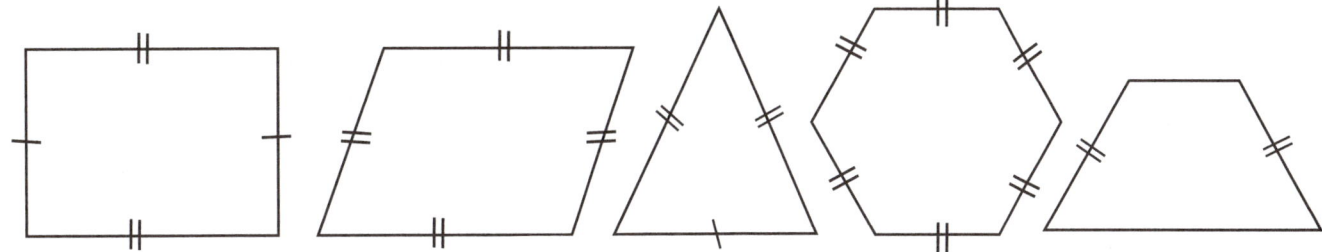

   _____   _____   _____   _____   _____

2. In your copy, for each shape, write the:

   (a) number of sides   (b) number of obtuse angles

   (c) number of angles   (d) lines of symmetry (vertical/horizontal)

   (e) number of acute angles

D. True or false?

1. A triangle with two equal sides is an isosceles triangle. ☐ true ☐ false
2. A parallelogram has four acute angles. ☐ true ☐ false
3. An equilateral triangle has three lines of symmetry. ☐ true ☐ false
4. A rhombus has four sides of equal length. ☐ true ☐ false
5. A right-angled triangle is a quadrilateral. ☐ true ☐ false
6. An equilateral triangle has one obtuse angle. ☐ true ☐ false
7. A four-sided shape with one pair of parallel lines is called a trapezium. ☐ true ☐ false
8. A square is a polygon and a quadrilateral. ☐ true ☐ false
9. Circles are good shapes for tessellating. ☐ true ☐ false

E. Real-life maths

1. Which letters have parallel lines?
   _____
2. Which letters have perpendicular lines?
   _____
3. Which letters have a vertical line of symmetry?
   _____
4. Which letters have a horizontal line of symmetry?
   _____
5. Do any letters have both horizontal and vertical lines of symmetry?
   _____

```
              A
   B    C    D    E    F
        G    H    I    J
             K    L    M
                  N    O
                  P
        Q    R    S    T    U
             V    W    X    Y
                  Z
```

Challenge yourself
Can you answer the same questions using numbers from 0 to 9?

F. Puzzle

How many diagonals has a regular octagon?

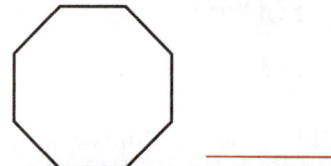

Test yourself!

1. **A parallelogram has:**
   - ☐ four acute angles
   - ☐ three acute and one obtuse angle
   - ☐ two acute and two obtuse angles
   - ☐ three obtuse and one acute angle

2. **A hexagon tessellates with:**
   - ☐ an octagon
   - ☐ a circle
   - ☐ a triangle
   - ☐ a square

3. **A rhombus has:**
   - ☐ one vertical line of symmetry
   - ☐ one horizontal line of symmetry
   - ☐ one vertical and one horizontal line of symmetry
   - ☐ no lines of symmetry

4. **A pentagon is:**
   - ☐ a quadrilateral
   - ☐ a polygon
   - ☐ a quadrilateral and a polygon
   - ☐ none of these

5. **An octagon has:**
   - ☐ no parallel lines
   - ☐ 2 pairs of parallel lines
   - ☐ 3 pairs of parallel lines
   - ☐ 4 pairs of parallel lines

6. **A right-angled triangle has:**
   - ☐ 1 right angle
   - ☐ 2 right angles
   - ☐ 3 right angles
   - ☐ No right angles

7. **The value of the angle at x is:**

   (Shape with angles 110°, x, 40°, 110°)

   - ☐ 110°
   - ☐ 260°
   - ☐ 40°
   - ☐ none of these

8. **A shape with four angles of 90° and 4 equal sides is:**
   - ☐ a rectangle
   - ☐ a square
   - ☐ a square or a rectangle
   - ☐ none of these

rough work

TOPIC 6 Division 1

A. Warm up!

Try these in your head.

1. 56 ÷ 8 = _____
2. 81 ÷ 9 = _____
3. 120 ÷ 10 = _____
4. 69 ÷ 7 = _____ R _____
5. 103 ÷ 9 = _____ R _____
6. 34 ÷ 16 = _____ R _____
7. 200 ÷ 10 = _____
8. 320 ÷ 20 = _____
9. 1,100 ÷ 100 = _____

B. In your mathematical opinion

The average distance from the surface of the Earth to the surface of the moon is 384,400km. A space shuttle travels at 28,000km per hour. Estimate how long it will take the space shuttle to travel to the moon. _____

C. Calculate!

Estimate and then find the answer to each of the followng using long division.

1. 133 ÷ 13
   estimate: _____
   answer: _____

2. 194 ÷ 20
   estimate: _____
   answer: _____

3. 199 ÷ 25
   estimate: _____
   answer: _____

4. 214 ÷ 17
   estimate: _____
   answer: _____

5. 418 ÷ 11
   estimate: _____
   answer: _____

6. 330 ÷ 22
   estimate: _____
   answer: _____

7. 417 ÷ 28
   estimate: _____
   answer: _____

8. 494 ÷ 26
   estimate: _____
   answer: _____

9. 612 ÷ 34
   estimate: _____
   answer: _____

D. Operations

Do you add, subtract, multiply or divide to find the answer?

1. Share 42 sweets equally among 21 people. _____
2. The sum of two numbers is 538. If one of the numbers is 74, what is the other number? _____
3. Make the number 12 two hundred times bigger. _____
4. The difference between two numbers is 201. One of the numbers is 114. What is the other number? _____
5. Make the number 484 twenty-two times smaller. _____

E. Real-life maths

This chart shows the amount of money raised at a cake sale.

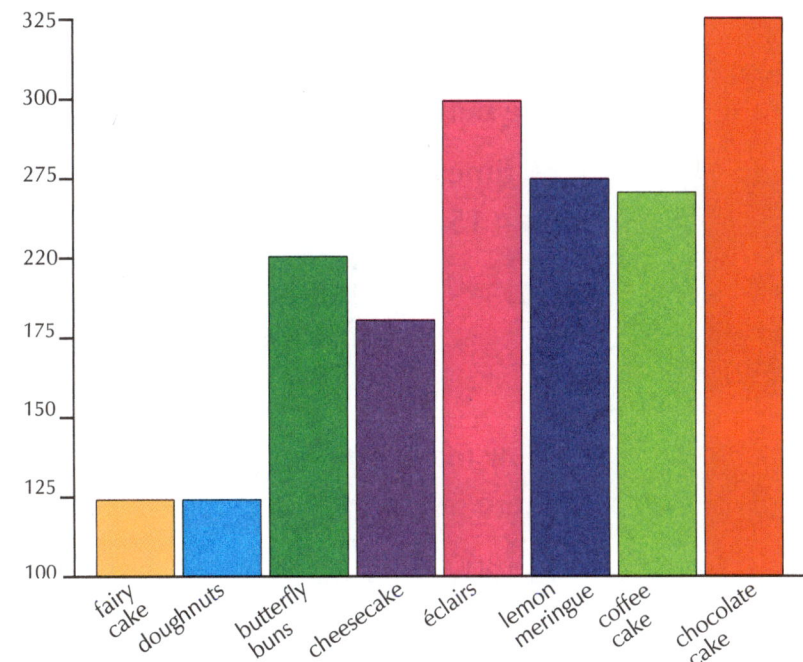

price list	price
fairy cake	€1·20
doughnut	60c
butterfly bun	€1·10
cheesecake	€11·00
éclair	90c
lemon meringue	€12·00
coffee/chocolate cake	€13·00

1. Which item made the most money? _____
2. How much less money did the éclairs bring in than the butterfly buns? _____
3. How many of each of the following were sold?

    (a) doughnuts _____   (b) cheesecakes _____   (c) lemon meringues _____
4. True or false? The same number of fairy cakes and doughnuts were sold. _____
5. Which type of cake, the chocolate or coffee, was most popular? _____
6. How much money did the cake sale make altogether? _____

Test yourself!

1. How many times can I take 72 from 792?
   - ☐ 792
   - ☐ 72
   - ☐ 10
   - ☐ 11

2. 15 x ___ = 255
   - ☐ 3,825
   - ☐ 17
   - ☐ 240
   - ☐ 13

3. 600 ÷ ___ = 25
   - ☐ 24
   - ☐ 25
   - ☐ 575
   - ☐ 625

4. 386 ÷ 52 = 5 R ___
   - ☐ 360
   - ☐ 146
   - ☐ 5
   - ☐ 26

5. 382 ÷ 37 = ___
   - ☐ 12 R 10
   - ☐ 10 R 12
   - ☐ 10
   - ☐ 12

6. ___ is 14 times smaller than 52.
   - ☐ 66
   - ☐ 38
   - ☐ 260
   - ☐ 728

rough work

7. Share 900 library books equally among 20 classrooms. They each get:
   - ☐ 880 books
   - ☐ 45 books
   - ☐ 20 books
   - ☐ 50 books

8. 919 apples must be put into bags of 12. How many will be left over?
   - ☐ 7
   - ☐ 76
   - ☐ 79
   - ☐ none

9. The number [ ] is 36 times plus 10 bigger than 15.
   - ☐ 540
   - ☐ 550
   - ☐ 61
   - ☐ 186

10. How many 50c are there in €300?
    - ☐ 300
    - ☐ 400
    - ☐ 500
    - ☐ 600

rough work

Topic 7: Fractions 1

A. Warm up!

Fill in the missing numerators and denominators.

1. $\frac{1}{2} = \frac{2}{\square}$
2. $\frac{2}{\square} = \frac{1}{5}$
3. $\frac{\square}{12} = \frac{3}{4}$
4. $\frac{5}{\square} = \frac{10}{12}$
5. $\frac{3}{\square} = \frac{6}{8}$
6. $\frac{\square}{3} = \frac{3}{9}$
7. $\frac{2}{3} = \frac{\square}{12}$
8. $\frac{3}{4} = \frac{0}{8} = \frac{\square}{12}$
9. $\frac{\square}{6} = \frac{2}{3}$
10. $\frac{2}{5} = \frac{4}{\square}$
11. $\frac{4}{\square} = \frac{8}{10}$
12. $\frac{2}{3} = \frac{\square}{6} = \frac{6}{\square} = \frac{8}{\square}$

B. In your mathematical opinion

What fraction of your day do you spend at each of these activities?

1. In school ☐
2. Eating (breakfast, lunch, dinner and snacks) ☐
3. Doing maths ☐
4. Sleeping ☐
5. Doing homework ☐

C. Operations

1. **Change each of the improper fractions to mixed numbers.**

   (a) $\frac{12}{5}$ ___
   (b) $\frac{5}{2}$ ___
   (c) $\frac{17}{4}$ ___
   (d) $\frac{13}{12}$ ___
   (e) $\frac{21}{10}$ ___
   (f) $\frac{14}{9}$ ___
   (g) $\frac{41}{3}$ ___
   (h) $\frac{23}{12}$ ___
   (i) $\frac{37}{5}$ ___
   (j) $\frac{19}{2}$ ___

2. **Change each of the following mixed numbers into improper fractions.**

   (a) $2\frac{1}{4}$ ___
   (b) $3\frac{1}{8}$ ___
   (c) $10\frac{1}{2}$ ___
   (d) $3\frac{2}{3}$ ___
   (e) $5\frac{3}{4}$ ___
   (f) $8\frac{2}{5}$ ___
   (g) $10\frac{3}{10}$ ___
   (h) $8\frac{5}{6}$ ___
   (i) $9\frac{3}{5}$ ___
   (j) $6\frac{7}{10}$ ___

3. **Label each of these as a common fraction, an improper fraction or a mixed number.**

   (a) $\frac{1}{2}$ _____
   (b) $\frac{7}{6}$ _____
   (c) $\frac{3}{3}$ _____
   (d) $1\frac{1}{4}$ _____
   (e) $\frac{17}{8}$ _____
   (f) $\frac{2}{5}$ _____

D. True or false?

1. $\frac{1}{2} < \frac{2}{3}$ ☐ true ☐ false
2. $\frac{2}{3} > \frac{3}{2}$ ☐ true ☐ false
3. $\frac{1}{5} = \frac{2}{10}$ ☐ true ☐ false
4. $\frac{14}{7} = 2$ ☐ true ☐ false
5. $\frac{3}{4} > \frac{9}{12}$ ☐ true ☐ false
6. $\frac{1}{5} > \frac{1}{3}$ ☐ true ☐ false
7. $\frac{2}{3} > \frac{5}{6}$ ☐ true ☐ false
8. $\frac{11}{12} = \frac{9}{10}$ ☐ true ☐ false
9. $\frac{3}{4} > \frac{4}{5}$ ☐ true ☐ false
10. $\frac{7}{8} = \frac{8}{9}$ ☐ true ☐ false

E. Real-life maths

Look at the final scores of the Wimbledon tennis finals.

men's final			
Tomas Havel, CZE	3	5	4
Rafael Lorca, ESP	6	7	6
ladies' final			
Serena Jones, USA	6	6	
Vera Plushenka, RUS	3	2	

1. Lorca was the winner of the men's final. ☐ true ☐ false
2. Havel won $\frac{4}{10}$ of the games in the last set. ☐ true ☐ false
3. Lorca won half of the games in the second set. ☐ true ☐ false
4. Lorca won $\frac{2}{3}$ of the games in the first set. ☐ true ☐ false
5. Overall, Havel won $\frac{12}{31}$ games. ☐ true ☐ false
6. Plushenka won the ladies' final. ☐ true ☐ false
7. Jones won $\frac{3}{4}$ of the games in the final set. ☐ true ☐ false
8. Plushenka won $\frac{1}{2}$ of the games in the first set. ☐ true ☐ false

F. Word puzzles

1. John got **five** out of **twelve** spellings correct in his spelling test. What fraction is that? ____
2. **Three** out of **ten** children in 5th Class are boys. ____
   (a) What fraction are boys? ____ (b) What fraction are girls? ____
3. James got €10 for his birthday. He spent €3 on a comic. What fraction has he left? ____
4. The Murphys had a pizza for lunch. Mum ate $\frac{1}{3}$, Dad ate $\frac{1}{4}$, Séan ate $\frac{1}{12}$ and Máire ate $\frac{1}{3}$. Put each person in order of how much they ate, starting with the person who had the least to eat. ___, ___, ___, ___

Test yourself!

1. The X on the number line shows ___.
   - [ ] $\frac{1}{2}$
   - [ ] $\frac{1}{3}$
   - [ ] $\frac{1}{4}$
   - [ ] $\frac{1}{5}$

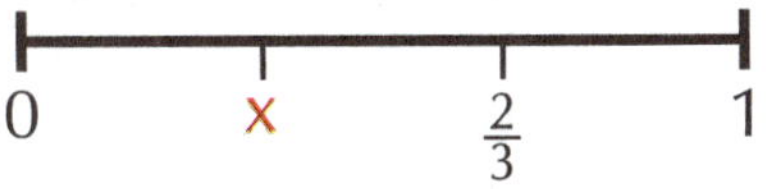

   0 —— X —— $\frac{2}{3}$ —— 1

2. $\frac{1}{3}$ is equivalent to:
   - [ ] $\frac{2}{4}$
   - [ ] $\frac{2}{6}$
   - [ ] $\frac{2}{8}$
   - [ ] $\frac{2}{10}$

3. $\frac{9}{12}$ is equivalent to:
   - [ ] $\frac{2}{3}$
   - [ ] $\frac{3}{4}$
   - [ ] $\frac{5}{6}$
   - [ ] $\frac{20}{24}$

4. The X on the number line shows:
   - [ ] $\frac{3}{4}$
   - [ ] $\frac{7}{8}$
   - [ ] $\frac{9}{10}$
   - [ ] $\frac{7}{9}$

   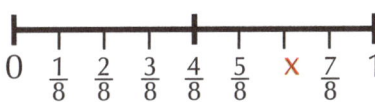

5. $\frac{11}{12} > $ ___.
   - [ ] $\frac{19}{20}$
   - [ ] $\frac{90}{100}$
   - [ ] $\frac{22}{24}$
   - [ ] $\frac{33}{30}$

6. How many halves are there in $5\frac{1}{2}$?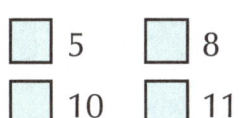
   - [ ] 5
   - [ ] 8
   - [ ] 10
   - [ ] 11

7. $\frac{20}{6}$ as a mixed number is:
   - [ ] $33\frac{1}{3}$
   - [ ] $3\frac{1}{3}$
   - [ ] $11\frac{1}{3}$
   - [ ] $7\frac{1}{3}$

8. $6\frac{2}{3}$ as an improper fraction is:
   - [ ] $\frac{23}{30}$
   - [ ] $\frac{11}{3}$
   - [ ] $\frac{3}{20}$
   - [ ] $\frac{20}{3}$

9. What fraction of €2 is 50c?
   - [ ] $\frac{1}{2}$
   - [ ] $\frac{1}{4}$
   - [ ] $\frac{1}{3}$
   - [ ] $\frac{1}{50}$

10. What fraction is represented by the X?
    - [ ] $1\frac{1}{3}$
    - [ ] $\frac{17}{12}$
    - [ ] $1\frac{1}{4}$
    - [ ] $1\frac{1}{2}$

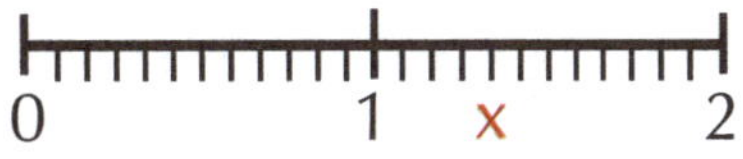

    0 —— 1 —— X —— 2

TOPIC 8 Fractions 2

A. Warm up!

Simplify the following fractions.

1. $\frac{2}{4}$ ___
2. $\frac{4}{6}$ ___
3. $\frac{2}{10}$ ___
4. $\frac{20}{40}$ ___
5. $\frac{4}{10}$ ___
6. $\frac{3}{12}$ ___
7. $\frac{8}{10}$ ___
8. $\frac{8}{12}$ ___
9. $\frac{15}{20}$ ___
10. $\frac{30}{100}$ ___
11. $\frac{30}{50}$ ___
12. $\frac{18}{20}$ ___

B. In your mathematical opinion

1. What fraction of people in your school are in 5th Class? ___
2. What fraction of the people in your class have curly hair? ___
3. What fraction of the people in your class are able to swim? ___
4. What fraction of your Maths book have you completed? ___

C. Calculate!

1. (a) $\frac{1}{2} + \frac{1}{4} =$ ___
   (b) $\frac{1}{3} + \frac{1}{6} =$ ___
   (c) $\frac{2}{3} + \frac{2}{3} =$ ___
   (d) $\frac{1}{12} + \frac{1}{4} =$ ___
   (e) $\frac{7}{10} + \frac{1}{5} =$ ___
   (f) $\frac{7}{9} + \frac{2}{3} =$ ___
   (g) $2\frac{1}{10} + 2\frac{4}{5} =$ ___
   (h) $3\frac{3}{4} + 1\frac{5}{8} =$ ___
   (i) $1\frac{9}{10} + 3\frac{2}{5} =$ ___

2. (a) $\frac{2}{3} - \frac{1}{3} =$ ___
   (b) $\frac{11}{12} - \frac{5}{12} =$ ___
   (c) $\frac{9}{10} - \frac{1}{5} =$ ___
   (d) $1\frac{1}{2} - 1\frac{1}{8} =$ ___
   (e) $3\frac{2}{3} - 1\frac{4}{9} =$ ___
   (f) $2\frac{1}{10} - \frac{9}{10} =$ ___
   (g) $4 - 2\frac{7}{12} =$ ___
   (h) $5\frac{1}{5} - 3\frac{7}{10} =$ ___
   (i) $5\frac{3}{4} - 2\frac{7}{8} =$ ___

3. (a) $\frac{1}{3} \times 3 =$ ___
   (b) $\frac{3}{4} \times 5 =$ ___
   (c) $\frac{1}{8} \times 10 =$ ___
   (d) $\frac{3}{10} \times 5 =$ ___
   (e) $\frac{7}{8} \times 6 =$ ___
   (f) $\frac{1}{2} \times 12 =$ ___
   (g) $\frac{9}{10} \times 4 =$ ___
   (h) $\frac{11}{12} \times 8 =$ ___
   (i) $\frac{19}{20} \times 5 =$ ___

D. True or false?

1. The sum of $\frac{3}{4}$ and $\frac{7}{8}$ is $\frac{13}{8}$. ☐ true ☐ false
2. The sum of 1 and $\frac{1}{2}$ is $\frac{4}{2}$. ☐ true ☐ false
3. The difference between $\frac{1}{2}$ and $\frac{1}{3}$ is $\frac{1}{6}$. ☐ true ☐ false
4. The difference between $\frac{1}{10}$ and $\frac{1}{5}$ is $\frac{1}{10}$. ☐ true ☐ false
5. 1 is two times bigger than $\frac{1}{2}$. ☐ true ☐ false
6. $1\frac{1}{4}$ is four times bigger than $\frac{1}{3}$. ☐ true ☐ false
7. $\frac{15}{10}$ simplified is $1\frac{1}{5}$. ☐ true ☐ false
8. There are 14 quarters in 3. ☐ true ☐ false

E. Real-life maths

A pet shop has the following animals in stock. Fill in the missing words.

| 1 parrot | 2 dogs | 6 hamsters | 3 cats | 4 rabbits | 8 goldfish |

1. $\frac{1}{12}$ of the animals in the pet shop are _____.
2. $\frac{1}{4}$ of the animals in the pet shop are _____.
3. _____ of the animals in the pet shop are cats.
4. $\frac{1}{3}$ of the animals in the pet shop are _____.
5. $\frac{7}{12}$ of the animals in the pet shop are either goldfish or _____.
6. Half of the animals in the pet shop are either rabbits or _____.

F. Word puzzles

1. Philip had €8. He spent $\frac{1}{8}$ of it. How much has he left? _____
2. $\frac{1}{4}$ of the people at a football match were children and $\frac{3}{10}$ were women. What fraction of the people at the match were men? ____
3. A farmer had **300** sheep. She sold $\frac{1}{5}$ of them. How many sheep had she left? ____
4. A carpenter had a plank of wood $2\frac{1}{4}$ metres long. He cut a $1\frac{1}{2}$-metre piece off the plank. How much is left? ____
5. Síle ran $4\frac{1}{5}$km on Saturday. On Sunday she ran $\frac{1}{2}$km farther. How far did she run over the two days? _____

Test yourself!

1. $\frac{3}{4} - \frac{1}{4} =$

   ☐ $\frac{1}{4}$ ☐ $\frac{1}{2}$
   ☐ 1 ☐ 0

2. $\frac{9}{12}$ in its simplest form is:

   ☐ $\frac{2}{3}$ ☐ $\frac{9}{1}$
   ☐ $\frac{3}{4}$ ☐ $\frac{18}{24}$

3. $\frac{2}{3} + \frac{2}{3} =$

   ☐ $\frac{2}{3}$ ☐ $\frac{4}{6}$
   ☐ $1\frac{1}{3}$ ☐ $1\frac{2}{3}$

4. $\frac{96}{108}$ in its simplest form is ___.

   ☐ $\frac{48}{54}$ ☐ $\frac{24}{27}$
   ☐ $\frac{8}{9}$ ☐ $\frac{192}{216}$

5. $2 - \frac{5}{8} =$ ___

   ☐ $1\frac{5}{8}$ ☐ $1\frac{3}{8}$
   ☐ $\frac{5}{8}$ ☐ $\frac{3}{8}$

6. $\frac{3}{8} + \frac{3}{4} =$

   ☐ $\frac{6}{12}$ ☐ $\frac{3}{4}$
   ☐ $\frac{1}{2}$ ☐ $1\frac{1}{8}$

7. $3\frac{9}{10} + 2\frac{4}{5} =$

   ☐ $6\frac{7}{10}$ ☐ $5\frac{13}{5}$
   ☐ $5\frac{13}{10}$ ☐ $1\frac{5}{10}$

8. A fraction equivalent to $\frac{50}{75}$ is:

   ☐ $5\frac{7}{5}$ ☐ $\frac{2}{3}$
   ☐ $5\frac{5}{7}$ ☐ $\frac{1}{15}$

9. $3\frac{1}{12} - 2\frac{2}{3} =$

   ☐ $1\frac{1}{9}$ ☐ $1\frac{3}{15}$
   ☐ $1\frac{5}{12}$ ☐ $\frac{5}{12}$

10. $\frac{7}{8} \times 4 =$

    ☐ $\frac{28}{32}$ ☐ $\frac{7}{32}$
    ☐ $\frac{28}{8}$ ☐ $1\frac{1}{2}$

TOPIC 9 Lines and Angles

A. Warm up!

Classify each of the following angles as acute, obtuse, right angle, straight, or reflex.

1.
2.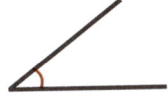
3.
4.

5.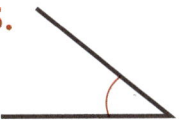
6.
7.
8.

B. In your mathematical opinion

1. What is the most frequently occurring angle in your classroom? _____
2. Can you think of a reason for this? _____

C. Calculate!

1. Estimate and measure each of these angles. Say what kind of angle each one is.

   (a)
   (b)
   (c)

   (d)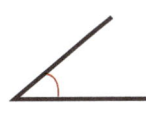
   (e)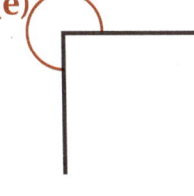
   (f)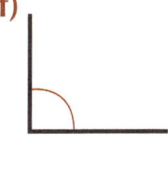

2. In your copy. Use your protractor to draw the following angles.

   (a) 130°   (b) 60°   (c) 30°   (d) 150°   (e) 210°   (f) 290°

D. True or false?

1. All the angles in a parallelogram are obtuse. ☐ true ☐ false
2. 91° is a right angle. ☐ true ☐ false
3. 100° is an obtuse angle. ☐ true ☐ false
4. The sum of the angles is a triangle is 200°. ☐ true ☐ false
5. An acute angle is > 0° and < 90°. ☐ true ☐ false
6. A full rotation is 300°. ☐ true ☐ false

E. Real-life maths

This is the dial on Sandra's dishwasher. The dial turns in a clockwise direction. How many degrees must Sandra turn the dial to do each of the following?

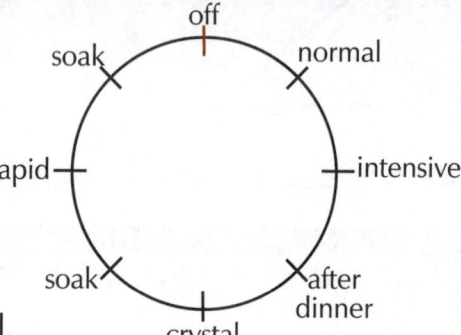

1. From off to intensive. _____
2. From off to normal. _____
3. From after dinner to off. _____
4. From rapid to off. _____
5. From normal to soak. _____
6. From off to crystal. _____
7. From off to rapid. _____
8. From normal to off. _____
9. From after dinner to rapid & dry. _____
10. From crystal to off to after dinner. _____

F. Measure

Measure the angles in each of the following shapes. What is the sum of the angles for each shape?

1.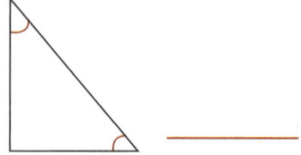

2.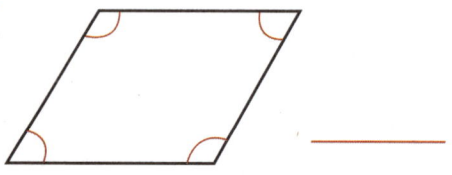

3.

4.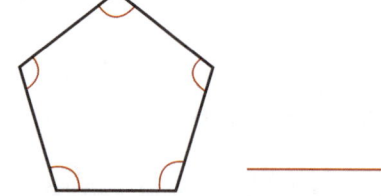

Test yourself!

1.

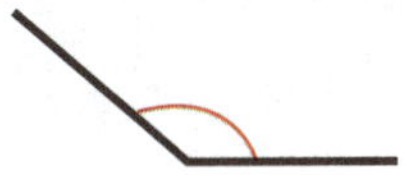

   This angle is:
   ☐ acute   ☐ right
   ☐ obtuse ☐ reflex

2.

   This angle is:
   ☐ acute   ☐ right
   ☐ obtuse ☐ reflex

3.

   This angle is:
   ☐ acute   ☐ right
   ☐ obtuse ☐ reflex

4. How many degrees is a full rotation?
   ☐ 90°   ☐ 80°
   ☐ 300°   ☐ 360°

5. What does the angle marked X measure?

   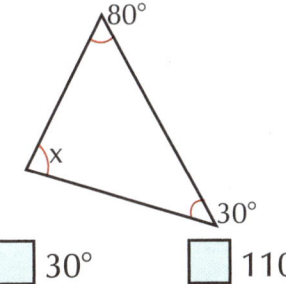

   ☐ 30°   ☐ 110°
   ☐ 180°   ☐ 70°

6. What does the angle marked X measure?

   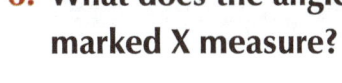

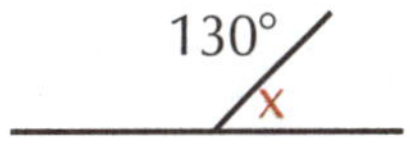

   ☐ 130°   ☐ 180°
   ☐ 50°   ☐ 70°

7. What does the angle marked X measure?

   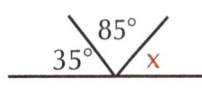

   ☐ 85°   ☐ 35°
   ☐ 120°   ☐ 60°

8. What does the angle marked X measure?

   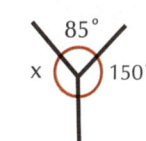

   ☐ 125°   ☐ 235°
   ☐ 85°   ☐ 150°

9. Use your protractor to measure this angle.

   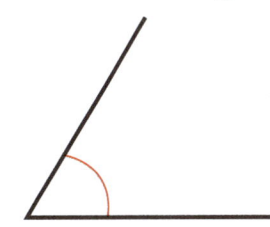

   ☐ 125°   ☐ 295°
   ☐ 65°   ☐ 70°

rough work

rough work

Planet Maths Activity Book • 5th Class

Topic 10 Decimals

A. Warm up!

Match each fraction with its decimal equivalent.

$\frac{1}{2}$ $\frac{1}{4}$ $\frac{7}{100}$ $\frac{67}{100}$ $\frac{1}{20}$ $\frac{1}{5}$ $\frac{9}{1000}$ $\frac{237}{1000}$

0·07   0·67   0·237   0·5   0·2   0·25   0·009   0·05

B. In your mathematical opinion

$\frac{1}{100}$ of a second = 10 milliseconds.

1. What is $\frac{1}{1000}$ of a second? _____
2. How many milliseconds in 10 seconds? _____
3. How many milliseconds in 1 minute? _____

C. Calculate!

1. Write these decimals as fractions or mixed numbers.

   (a) 0·067 ___   (b) 0·003 ___   (c) 0·017 ___   (d) 0·747 ___   (e) 2·307 ___
   (f) 5·049 ___   (g) 3·001 ___   (h) 4·040 ___   (i) 12·051 ___   (j) 14·404 ___

2. Write these fractions as decimals.

   (a) $\frac{6}{1000}$ ___   (b) $\frac{11}{1000}$ ___   (c) $\frac{61}{1000}$ ___   (d) $\frac{124}{1000}$ ___   (e) $\frac{227}{1000}$ ___
   (f) $\frac{300}{1000}$ ___   (g) $\frac{750}{1000}$ ___   (h) $\frac{1200}{1000}$ ___   (i) $\frac{1250}{1000}$ ___   (j) $\frac{2500}{1000}$ ___

3. Write each of these decimals in extended form, e.g. 0.624 = 6 tenths + 2 hundredths + 4 thousandths.

   (a) 0·021 = _____
   (b) 0·149 = _____
   (c) 0·508 = _____

D. True or false?

1. 0·1 can be taken from 1·0 ten times.   □ true □ false
2. 0·25 + 0·25 = 5·0   □ true □ false
3. $\frac{1}{1000}$ is one thousand times less than 1 unit.   □ true □ false
4. $\frac{4}{5}$ as a decimal is 0·45.   □ true □ false
5. $1 - \frac{1}{5} = 0\cdot 8$ □ true □ false
6. $0\cdot 606 < \frac{606}{1000}$ □ true □ false

E. Real-life maths

This table shows how many kilometres each animal can run in 1 minute.

antelope	1·63 kilometres per minute
cheetah	1·88 kilometres per minute
coyote	1·15 kilometres per minute
elk	1·2 kilometres per minute
lion	1·33 kilometres per minute

1. Which of these animals can travel the fastest? _____
2. Which is the slowest animal in the group? _____
3. How far will an antelope travel in 2 minutes? _____
4. How far will an elk travel in 5 minutes? _____
5. Can a cheetah run 10km in 5 minutes? _____
6. To the nearest kilometre, how far can the lion travel in 10 minutes? _____

F. Word puzzles

1. A suitcase weighs **15·25kg** and a bag weighs **1·06kg**.
   How much heavier is the suitcase? _____
2. The distance between two houses is **0·045km**. If you walked back and forth between the houses 5 times, how far would you have travelled? _____
3. A bottle of nail polish is **€7·99** and a bottle of nail varnish remover is **€1·89**. If I bought both products how much change would I have from **€20**? _____
4. A teaspoon can hold **0·005 litres** of water and a cup can hold **0·3 litres** of water. How much more can the cup hold? _____

Test yourself!

1. The value of the underlined number in 3·4<u>2</u>6 is:
   - ☐ 2 units
   - ☐ 2 hundreds
   - ☐ 2 hundredths
   - ☐ 2 thousandths

2. How much less than 2 is 1·044?
   - ☐ 0·956
   - ☐ 1·956
   - ☐ 9·560
   - ☐ 96·5

3. The value of the underlined digit in 0·11<u>8</u> is:
   - ☐ 8
   - ☐ 8,000
   - ☐ $\frac{8}{100}$
   - ☐ $\frac{8}{1000}$

4. How much greater than 5 is 2·060?
   - ☐ 7·060
   - ☐ 29·4
   - ☐ 294
   - ☐ 2·94

5. $\frac{3}{5}$ is the same as:
   - ☐ 0·35
   - ☐ 0·55
   - ☐ 0·65
   - ☐ 0·6

6. $1\frac{7}{1000}$ is the same as:
   - ☐ 17 thousands
   - ☐ 17 thousandths
   - ☐ 1 unit and 7 hundreds
   - ☐ 1 unit and 7 thousandths

7. The value of the underlined number in 3·<u>3</u>44 is:
   - ☐ $\frac{3}{1000}$
   - ☐ 3
   - ☐ $\frac{3}{100}$
   - ☐ $\frac{3}{10}$

8. The difference between 0·5 kg and 6 kg is:
   - ☐ 1kg
   - ☐ 0.5kg
   - ☐ 5.5kg
   - ☐ 0.56kg

9. $\frac{4}{1000} + 3 + \frac{9}{100} + \frac{2}{10} =$ ___
   - ☐ 4.392
   - ☐ 3.942
   - ☐ 3.294
   - ☐ 3.492

10. 10·001 is how much greater than 1?
    - ☐ $\frac{1}{10}$
    - ☐ $\frac{1}{100}$
    - ☐ $\frac{1}{1000}$
    - ☐ 1

TOPIC 11 Problem Solving

A. Warm up!

1. It was the first day of soccer practice. The coach suggested that it would be a good idea for every child to meet every other child at the practice. The coach said, "When you meet, please shake hands and tell each other your names."
   If there were 12 children at soccer practice, how many handshakes were there? _____

2. A shed can be built by 5 men in 25 days. After 10 days, 10 more men start working on the job. How many days are now required to build the shed? _____

B. Fraction puzzles

(a)  (b)  (c)  (d)

(e)  (f)  (g)  (h)

1. What fraction of each tile above is black?

   (a) ___   (b) ___   (c) ___   (d) ___
   (e) ___   (f) ___   (g) ___   (h) ___

2. What fraction of each tile above is white?

   (a) ___   (b) ___   (c) ___   (d) ___
   (e) ___   (f) ___   (g) ___   (h) ___

3. Combine the tiles to make these fractions and mixed numbers.
   e.g. Using the black areas, [tile a] + [tile d] = $\frac{12}{8}$ = $1\frac{4}{8}$ = $1\frac{1}{2}$

   (a) $\frac{7}{8}$ _____   (b) $\frac{5}{8}$ _____   (c) $1\frac{1}{8}$ _____   (d) $1\frac{1}{4}$ _____
   (e) $1\frac{1}{2}$ _____   (f) $1\frac{3}{8}$ _____   (g) $\frac{1}{8}$ _____   (h) $\frac{1}{4}$ _____

C. Word puzzles

1. There are **2** letters and **6** numbers on a number plate.
   How many letters and numbers are on 8 number plates? _____

2. A ship left Dublin to sail to Calais at **21:20**. It arrived in Calais at a **quarter past eight** the following morning.
   If the ship was 17 minutes early, how long should the journey have taken? _____

3. Gearóid scored **77** out of a possible **110** in his Maths test. What fraction of the questions did he not get? _____

D. Now try these

1. The temperature at midnight is ⁻10 °C. It rises by 0·5°C every hour after midnight. What is the temperature at midday? _____

2. What number am I?
   I am a multiple of 7.
   Both my digits are even.
   The difference between my digits in 4.
   _____

3. How many dots will there be in the twentieth triangle? _____

1st **2nd** **3rd**

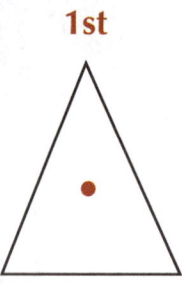 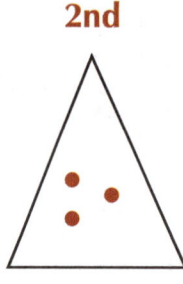 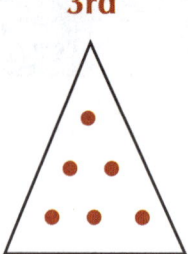

F. Puzzle

There are 21 candles in a church. When a candle reduces to $\frac{1}{7}$ of its original size it gets too small to burn, so the priest puts it aside. But the priest hates to waste things, so when he realises that he has enough of these small pieces to join and make another candle the same size, he joins them and uses the new candle. He uses one candle each day. How many days would 21 candles last? _____

Test yourself!

1. **1, 4, 9, 16** What number comes next in the sequence?
   - ☐ 19
   - ☐ 25
   - ☐ 36
   - ☐ 27

2. Banana is to apple as potato is to:
   - ☐ lettuce
   - ☐ cabbage
   - ☐ carrot
   - ☐ broccoli

3. **1, 10, 3, 9, 5, 8, 7, 7, 9, 6** What are the next two numbers in the sequence?
   - ☐ 3, 3
   - ☐ 11, 5
   - ☐ 5, 11
   - ☐ 13, 11

4. Four years ago, Siobhán was twice as old as Liam. Four years from now, Liam will be $\frac{3}{4}$ of Siobhán's age. How old is Siobhán now?
   - ☐ 10
   - ☐ 12
   - ☐ 16
   - ☐ 24

5. **2, 3, 5, 7, ___, 17** What number is missing in this sequence?
   - ☐ 9
   - ☐ 11
   - ☐ 15
   - ☐ 12

6. **Z, A, Y, B, X, C, W** What are the next two letters in this sequence?
   - ☐ U, F
   - ☐ V, D
   - ☐ D, V
   - ☐ V, E

7. What is the number that is one half of one-quarter of one-tenth of 800?
   - ☐ 80
   - ☐ 40
   - ☐ 20
   - ☐ 10

8. If you count from 1 to 100, how many 9s will you pass on the way
   - ☐ 10
   - ☐ 11
   - ☐ 20
   - ☐ 21

9. What is the next number in this sequence?
   0, 1, 1, 2, 3, 5, 8, 13, 21
   - ☐ 31
   - ☐ 34
   - ☐ 35
   - ☐ 41

rough work

rough work

TOPIC 12 Number Theory?

A. Warm up!

Say whether each of these numbers is odd or even *and* **prime or composite**.

1. 2 _____, _____
2. 6 _____, _____
3. 11 _____, _____
4. 15 _____, _____
5. 18 _____, _____
6. 21 _____, _____

B. In your mathematical opinion

Estimate and then investigate which of the following has the greatest number of factors.

1. 9 or 10
2. 12 or 25
3. 36 or 42
4. 48 or 56

B. Calculate!

1. Write the first five multiples for each of these numbers.

   (a) 5 ___, ___, ___, ___, ___
   (b) 8 ___, ___, ___, ___, ___
   (c) 12 ___, ___, ___, ___, ___
   (d) 16 ___, ___, ___, ___, ___
   (e) 20 ___, ___, ___, ___, ___
   (f) 18 ___, ___, ___, ___, ___

2. List the factors for each of these numbers.

   (a) 6 _____
   (b) 8 _____
   (c) 14 _____
   (d) 20 _____
   (e) 24 _____
   (f) 37 _____

3. What is the product for each of these pairs of numbers?

   (a) 2 and 7 _____
   (b) 4 and 5 _____
   (c) 3 and 8 _____
   (d) 9 and 4 _____
   (e) 8 and 12 _____
   (f) 9 and 13 _____

C. True or false?

1. 4 is a multiple of 2. ☐ true ☐ false
2. 6 is a multiple of 4 and 2. ☐ true ☐ false
3. The first three multiples of 7 are 7, 14 and 21. ☐ true ☐ false
4. 2 is an even number. ☐ true ☐ false
5. 2 is a composite number. ☐ true ☐ false
6. 21 is an odd and a composite number. ☐ true ☐ false
7. 24 is a square number. ☐ true ☐ false
8. 20 is a rectangular number. ☐ true ☐ false

D. Fill in the missing words

1. A _____ number has no factors other than 1 and itself.
2. A _____ is a whole number that divides into another number with no remainder.
3. When I add two even numbers I always get an _____ number.
4. Pairs of factors have a _____.
5. When I add an even and _____ number, I get an odd number.
6. An even number always ends in ___, 2, ___, ___ or 8.
7. When I multiply two _____ numbers, I always get an _____ number.
8. The _____ factor of 10 is 10.
9. _____ is the third square number.
10. 16 is the _____ square number.

E. Word puzzles

1. There is going to be a meeting in the town hall. The caretaker has to arrange **50** chairs so that there is an equal number of chairs in each row. How many different ways can he do this? In your copy, show your answers and draw diagrams.

2. For another meeting the caretaker has to put out **70** chairs. This time there needs to be the same number of chairs in every row and every column.

    (a) Can the caretaker do this with 70 chairs? _____

    (b) With 70 chairs, what is the highest number he can arrange in a perfect square? _____

Test yourself!

1. An even number is always divisible by:
   - [ ] 1
   - [ ] 2
   - [ ] 3
   - [ ] 4

2. An odd number is never divisible by:
   - [ ] 1
   - [ ] 2
   - [ ] 3
   - [ ] 4

3. Which of these is a factor of 5?
   - [ ] 5
   - [ ] 10
   - [ ] 15
   - [ ] 20

4. Which of these is a product of 3 and 4?
   - [ ] 1
   - [ ] 7
   - [ ] 12
   - [ ] 34

5. Which of these is a multiple of 25?
   - [ ] 15
   - [ ] 20
   - [ ] 25
   - [ ] 30

6. Which of these is a square number?
   - [ ] 4
   - [ ] 6
   - [ ] 8
   - [ ] 10

7. The fourth square number is:
   - [ ] 4
   - [ ] 1
   - [ ] 9
   - [ ] 16

8. Which of these is an example of a prime number?
   - [ ] 21
   - [ ] 22
   - [ ] 23
   - [ ] 24

9. Which of these is an example of a composite number?
   - [ ] 1
   - [ ] 2
   - [ ] 3
   - [ ] 4

10. If children could be arranged in equal groups of 2, 4, 6 or 8, what is the least number of children there could be?
    - [ ] 16
    - [ ] 20
    - [ ] 24
    - [ ] 28

rough work

rough work

Topic 13: Multiplication 2

A. Warm up

Make each of these numbers 10 times bigger.

1. 2 ____
2. 30 ____
3. 110 ____
4. 2·6 ____
5. 4·08 ____
6. 5·55 ____
7. 17·2 ____
8. 22·48 ____
9. 118·76 ____
10. 244·982 ____

B. In your mathematical opinion

0   1   2   3   4   5

Using the numbers above, how many different decimal numbers combinations can you make?

☐ · ☐ ☐ ☐

C. Calculate!

1. Round each of the following to the nearest whole number.

   (a) 1·2 ____
   (b) 2·9 ____
   (c) 13·98 ____
   (d) 25·56 ____
   (e) 52·08 ____
   (f) 60·514 ____
   (g) 64·095 ____
   (h) 112·66 ____
   (i) 204·911 ____

2. Estimate the answers to each of the following.

   (a) 2·6 x 8 = ____
   (b) 3·4 x 9 = ____
   (c) 10·4 x 5 = ____
   (d) 3·44 x 8 = ____
   (e) 10·49 x 9 = ____
   (f) 12·114 x 6 = ____

3. Estimate and then find the answers to each of the following.

   (a) 0·94 x 8 = ____, ____
   (b) 0·886 x 7 = ____, ____
   (c) 2·429 x 9 = ____, ____
   (d) 5·014 x 9 = ____, ____
   (e) 7·559 x 12 = ____, ____
   (f) 9·046 x 10 = ____, ____

Based on Planet Maths 5 pages 85, 86, 87 and 89

D. True or false?

1. 1·2 > 1·092. ☐ true ☐ false
2. 4·095 to the nearest whole number is 5. ☐ true ☐ false
3. 14 is 10 times bigger than 1·4. ☐ true ☐ false
4. 11·06 is 10 times bigger than 1·106. ☐ true ☐ false
5. 2·479 x 9 is 223·11. ☐ true ☐ false
6. A reasonable estimate for 1·138 x 8 is 9. ☐ true ☐ false
7. A reasonable estimate for 12·068 x 10 is 1,200. ☐ true ☐ false
8. 138·95 is 25 times bigger than 5·558. ☐ true ☐ false

E. Real life maths

Gravity is the force that pulls things together. Something that weighs 1kg on Earth weighs 2·36kg on Jupiter and 1·13kg on Neptune.

Calculate the weight of each of these people on Jupiter and Neptune.

Name	Sinéad	William	James	Deirdre	Áine
weight	53kg	51kg	45kg	61kg	49kg
on Jupiter					
on Neptune					

F. Word puzzles

1. Carlos can run **1km** in **5·5** minutes. How long will it take him to run **10km** if he keeps the same speed? _____
2. A bag of parsnips weighs **0·783kg**. A bag of carrots is **four** times heavier. What is the weight of the bag of carrots? _____
3. The distance from the school to the local church is **0·045km**. A class walked to the church and back **seven** times in one term. How far did they walk? _____
4. A boy is **42** times heavier than his pet parrot. His parrot weighs **0·143kg**. What is the weight of the boy? How many kilograms more then the parrot does he weigh? _____
5. A water tank can hold **fifty-two** times more water than a bucket. The capacity of the bucket is **4·362 litres**. What is the capacity of the water tank? _____

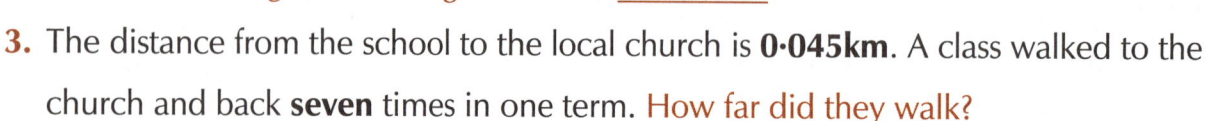

Test yourself!

1. 0·785 rounded to the nearest whole number is:
   - [ ] 0
   - [ ] 1
   - [ ] 78.5
   - [ ] 2

2. 4·506 rounded to the nearest whole number is:
   - [ ] 4
   - [ ] 5
   - [ ] 45
   - [ ] 450

3. 107·096 rounded to the nearest whole number is:
   - [ ] 107
   - [ ] 108
   - [ ] 107.09
   - [ ] 108.09

4. A reasonable estimate for 2·386 x 14 is:
   - [ ] 280
   - [ ] 28
   - [ ] 23
   - [ ] 238

5. A reasonable estimate for 25·179 x 10 is:
   - [ ] 25
   - [ ] 250
   - [ ] 2,500
   - [ ] 2,570

6. 2·874 x 24 =
   - [ ] 48
   - [ ] 6·879
   - [ ] 689·76
   - [ ] 68·976

7. 12·948 x 20 =
   - [ ] 240
   - [ ] 258·96
   - [ ] 25·896
   - [ ] 2,589·6

8. The school bus travels 6·755km on 1 litre of petrol. How far will it travel on 30 litres of petrol?
   - [ ] 20·265km
   - [ ] 202·65km
   - [ ] 23·245km
   - [ ] 0·225km

9. A box contains 28 mobile phones. If each phone weighs 0·985kg, what is the total weight of the content of the box?
   - [ ] 27·58kg
   - [ ] 28·985kg
   - [ ] 2·758kg
   - [ ] 275·8kg

10. A rice cake weighs 0·009kg. There are 14 rice cakes in a packet and 35 packets in a box. What is the total weight of contents of the box?
    - [ ] 0·126kg
    - [ ] 12·6kg
    - [ ] 44·1kg
    - [ ] 4·41kg

rough work

rough work

Topic 14: Length

A. Warm up!

Write each of these lengths in millimetres.

1. 5 cm _____
2. 12 cm _____
3. $6\frac{1}{2}$ cm _____
4. $30\frac{1}{2}$ cm _____
5. 90 cm _____
6. 9 cm 4 mm _____
7. 14·3 cm _____
8. 29·4 cm _____

B. In your mathematical opinion

1. Measure the length of your step. _____
2. How far would you walk if you took:

    (a) 10 steps _____
    (b) 100 steps _____
    (c) 1,000 steps _____

C. Calculate!

1. **Write the following as centimetres using the decimal point.**

    (a) 7mm _____
    (b) 9mm _____
    (c) 15mm _____
    (d) 37mm _____
    (e) 128mm _____
    (f) 256mm _____
    (g) 7cm 4mm _____
    (h) 28cm 4mm _____

2. **Write the following as metres using the decimal point.**

    (a) 85cm _____
    (b) 99cm _____
    (c) 113cm _____
    (d) 234cm _____
    (e) 583cm _____
    (f) 1,162cm _____
    (g) 2m 86cm _____
    (h) 4m 55cm _____

3. **Write the following as kilometres using the decimal point.**

    (a) 5m _____
    (b) 66m _____
    (c) 138m _____
    (d) 673m _____
    (e) 2,685m _____
    (f) 7km 500m _____
    (g) 9km 60m _____
    (h) $10\frac{1}{4}$ km _____

4. **Calculate the following distance sums.**

    (a) 23mm + 5cm + 4m = _____
    (b) $3\frac{1}{2}$m + 26cm + 7mm = _____
    (c) 2km + $1\frac{1}{4}$m + 9cm = _____
    (d) 3km 400m + 23m + 17cm = _____

D. True or false?

1. The perimeter of a square with a side of 4m is 16m. ☐ true ☐ false
2. There are 550mm in 55cm. ☐ true ☐ false
3. $7\frac{1}{2}$ km is equal to 750m. ☐ true ☐ false
4. The perimeter of a regular hexagon with a side of 6m is 36m. ☐ true ☐ false
5. $1\frac{3}{4}$m is equivalent to 175cm. ☐ true ☐ false
6. 3km 4m is equivalent to 3·4km. ☐ true ☐ false
7. 1,268mm is equivalent to 1·268m. ☐ true ☐ false

E. Real-life maths

1. What is the length of the perimeter of your school playground? Estimate first and then measure it.   estimate: ___   measure: ___
2. How long does it take you to walk around the playground? _____
3. How many times would you have to walk around it to travel these distances?
   (a) 1km _____   (b) 5km _____   (c) 10km _____
4. How long would it take you to complete these journeys?
   (a) _____   (b) _____   (c) _____

F. Word puzzles

1. A man is **170cm** tall. His wife is **1·52 metres** tall. What is the difference between them?
   _____
2. The perimeter of a square is **52 metres**. What is the length of each side?
3. Máire set off on a walk **3km 650m** long. After an hour she had walked **2·95km**. How far has she still to walk? _____
4. A length of rope **7·15** metres long was cut into 5 equal sections. What was the length of each piece? _____
5. A rectangle has a perimeter of **26m**. The length of the rectangle is **9m**. What is its width? _____
6. Jack walked **2·25km** and Sile walked **$1\frac{1}{4}$m** farther than Jack. What distance did Sile cover? _____

Test yourself!

1. 67 mm is equivalent to:
   - ☐ 67cm
   - ☐ 670cm
   - ☐ $6\frac{7}{10}$cm
   - ☐ 0·67cm

2. $10\frac{1}{5}$ cm is equivalent to:
   - ☐ 10cm 5mm
   - ☐ 10cm 2mm
   - ☐ 150mm
   - ☐ 120mm

3. How many kilometres in 2,500 metres?
   - ☐ 2·5km
   - ☐ 25km
   - ☐ 250km
   - ☐ $2\frac{1}{5}$ km

4. An appropriate measuring instrument for finding the length of a nail is:
   - ☐ a metre stick
   - ☐ a trundle wheel
   - ☐ a mm ruler
   - ☐ a measuring tape

5. An appropriate measuring instrument for finding the length of your arm is:
   - ☐ a metre stick
   - ☐ a trundle wheel
   - ☐ a mm ruler
   - ☐ a measuring tape

6. An appropriate unit of measurement for finding the width of a €1 coin is:
   - ☐ millimetres
   - ☐ centimetres
   - ☐ metres
   - ☐ kilometres

7. An appropriate unit of measurement for finding the distance between two cities is:
   - ☐ millimetres
   - ☐ centimetres
   - ☐ metres
   - ☐ kilometres

8. The perimeter of a square with a side of $4\frac{1}{4}$ metres is:
   - ☐ 8.5 metres
   - ☐ 17 metres
   - ☐ 12·75 metres
   - ☐ 425 centimetres

9. The perimeter of a rectangle is 30m. What is its length?
   - ☐ 5m
   - ☐ 20m
   - ☐ 10m
   - ☐ 15m

rough work

rough work

46 Planet Maths Activity Book • 5th Class

Topic 15: Division of Decimals

A. Warm up!

Make each of these numbers ten times smaller.

1. 120 ____
2. 50 ____
3. 1,230 ____
4. 2,050 ____
5. 5,025 ____
6. 55 ____
7. 72 ____
8. 12 ____
9. 9 ____
10. 2 ____

B. In your mathematical opinion

On average you inhale 0·58 litres of air when you breathe in.

1. How many breaths do you inhale in one minute? ___
2. How many litres of air is that? ___
3. How much air do you inhale in 1 hour? ___
4. What about 1 day? ___
5. What about 1 week? ___

C. Calculate!

1. (a) 594 ÷ 22 = ___   (b) 315 ÷ 21 = ___   (c) 756 ÷ 63 = ___
   (d) 767 ÷ 59 = ___   (e) 924 ÷ 84 = ___   (f) 972 ÷ 81 = ___

2. (a) 52·7 ÷ 7 = ___   (b) 42·4 ÷ 8 = ___   (c) 26·1 ÷ 9 = ___
   (d) 25·8 ÷ 6 = ___   (e) 12·8 ÷ 8 = ___
   (f) 48·3 ÷ 7 = ___

3. (a) 9·32 ÷ 4 = ___   (b) 7·84 ÷ 4 = ___
   (c) 3·42 ÷ 9 = ___   (d) 1·96 ÷ 7 = ___
   (e) 2·79 ÷ 9 = ___   (f) 5·04 ÷ 8 = ___

D. True or false?

1. 2,500 is ten times larger than 25. ☐ true ☐ false
2. The number that is 10 times smaller than 25 is 0·25. ☐ true ☐ false
3. The difference between the underlined digits in 87·798 and 0·074 is 63. ☐ true ☐ false
4. 4 divided by 10 is 0.04. ☐ true ☐ false
5. 8 divided by 100 is 0.08. ☐ true ☐ false
6. The number that is 10 times smaller than 0·12 is 0·012. ☐ true ☐ false
7. The number that is 100 times smaller than 21·45 is 2·145. ☐ true ☐ false
8. 1·497 is 10 times bigger than 14·97. ☐ true ☐ false

E. Real-life maths

Usain Bolt from Jamaica had a world record for running 100 metres in 9·56 seconds.

1. Could he run 10 metres in 1 second or less? ___
2. How long would it take him to run 1,000 metres if he ran at that speed all the time? ___
3. How long would it take him to run 10km if he ran at that speed all the time? ___

F. Word puzzles

For each question, say whether you add, subtract, multiply or divide. Then, solve the quzzles.

1. **46·8kg** of flour was shared equally among **eighteen** students. How much did they each receive? _____
2. Julie walked **50·4km** over a period of **14** days. On average, how far did she walk each day? _____
3. **1·44** litres of water was poured in **15** bottles. How much water in total was that? _____
4. **Thirty-two** phone books were laid end to end. Altogether, the length of the books was **1·56m**. How long is each phone book? _____
5. **22** men built a wall **2·12km** in length. On average, what length of the wall did they each build? _____

Test yourself!

1. 810 ÷ 45 =

   ☐ 18   ☐ 765
   ☐ 855 ☐ 28

2. 706 ÷ 83 =

   ☐ 4 R 82   ☐ 2 R 84
   ☐ 8 R 42   ☐ 8 R 24

3. 25 x ____ = 34

   ☐ 1·6   ☐ 3·1
   ☐ 6·13   ☐ 1·36

4. 0·055 is ____ times smaller than 55.

   ☐ 10   ☐ 100
   ☐ 1,000 ☐ 10,000

5. 2·16 is ____ times bigger than 0·216.

   ☐ 10   ☐ 100
   ☐ 1,000 ☐ 10,000

6. The difference between 0·08 and 0·008 is:

   ☐ 72   ☐ 7·2
   ☐ 0·72 ☐ 0·072

rough work

7. How many times is 23 contained in 37·72?

   ☐ 16·4 ☐ 164
   ☐ 1·64 ☐ 0·164

8. What number is 1,000 times bigger than 0·047?

   ☐ 47   ☐ 470
   ☐ 4,700 ☐ 47,000

9. $\frac{44.03}{17}$ =

   ☐ 25·9   ☐ 2·59
   ☐ 0·259 ☐ 259

10. Share €31·75 among 25 people. They each get:

    ☐ €12·70 ☐ €1·27
    ☐ 27c   ☐ 12·7c

rough work

TOPIC 16: Time

A. Warm up!

1. Write these minutes as hours and minutes.
   - (a) 82 mins ___
   - (b) 96 mins ___
   - (c) 100 mins ___
   - (d) 125 mins ___
   - (e) 185 mins ___
   - (f) 250 mins ___

2. Write these hours and minutes as minutes.
   - (a) 1h 25m ___
   - (b) 1h 45m ___
   - (c) 2h 05m ___
   - (d) 2h 55m ___
   - (e) 3h 10m ___
   - (f) 5h 22m ___

B. In your mathematical opinion

1. How long do you spend sleeping each night? ___
2. How many hours is that each week? ___
3. How many hours is that each year? ___
4. If you live until you are 78, how much of your life will you spend sleeping? ___
   Can you write your answer in years and days? ___ years ___ days

C. Calculate!

1. Write each of the digital times using the 24-hour clock system.
   - (a) 11:25 am _____
   - (b) midnight _____
   - (c) 9:25 pm _____
   - (d) 5:30 pm _____
   - (e) 6:20 am _____
   - (f) 7:55 pm _____
   - (g) 4:15 pm _____
   - (h) midday _____

2. Write each of the 24-hour times using am or pm.
   - (a) 08:35 _____
   - (b) 19:50 _____
   - (c) 18:25 _____
   - (d) 17:07 _____
   - (e) 20:12 _____
   - (f) 07:05 _____
   - (g) 23:42 _____
   - (h) 00:30 _____

3. Write each of these analogue times using the 24-hour clock.
   - (a) 5 to 9 in the morning _____
   - (b) 25 past 11 at night _____
   - (c) Half past ten in the morning _____
   - (d) A quarter past 4 in the afternoon _____

D. True or false?

1. 5 past midnight is the same as 00:05. ☐ true ☐ false
2. There are 90 minutes in $1\frac{1}{2}$ hours. ☐ true ☐ false
3. The length of time from 11:42 to 14:05 is 2 hours 20 minutes. ☐ true ☐ false
4. $\frac{3}{4}$ of an hour is 75 minutes. ☐ true ☐ false
5. There are 75 minutes in $1\frac{1}{4}$ hours. ☐ true ☐ false
6. $2\frac{1}{2}$ hours after 21:15 is 23:45. ☐ true ☐ false
7. 2 h 34 m + 1 h 15 m + 2 h 26 m = 6 h 15 m ☐ true ☐ false
8. 3·5 hours is 3 hours and 50 minutes. ☐ true ☐ false

E. Real-life maths

Train timetable for Westport & Ballina to Dublin Heuston. (Monday to Saturday)

		Mon to Fri	Mon to Sat	Mon to Sat	Mon to Sat
Westport	Dep	05:15	07:15	13:15	17:45
Castlebar	Dep	05:27	07:27	13:27	17:57
Manulla Junction	Arr	...	07:35	13:35	18:05
Manulla Junction	Dep	...	07:35	13:35	18:05
Claremorris	Dep	05:47	07:50	13:52	18:22
Ballyhaunis	Dep	06:00	08:03	14:05	18:35
Castlerea	Dep	06:15	08:18	14:20	18:50
Roscommon	Dep	06:35	08:38	14:40	19:10
Athlone	Arr	07:00	09:03	15:06	19:35
Athlone	Dep	07:05	09:03	15:06	19:35
Clara	Dep	07:21	09:22	15:30	19:59
Tullamore	Dep	07:31	09:31	15:39	20:08
Portarlington	Dep	07:54	09:51	15:59	20:28
Monasterevin	Dep	08:00	...	...	...
Kildare	Dep	08:10	...	16:12	...
Newbridge	Dep	08:18	...	...	...
Dublin Heuston	Arr	08:50	10:45	16:50	21:20

1. How many trains are there each day from Westport to Dublin Heuston? ___
2. Does each train take the same length of time to go from Westport to Dublin? ___
3. A train departs Westport at 07:15. How long does it take to reach Athlone? ___
4. If a passenger wanted to go from Westport to Monasterevin, which train do they need to get? ___
5. A passenger needs to be in Dublin city centre for a meeting at 2pm. Which train should they get from Tullamore? ___

Test yourself!

1. 89 minutes is equal to:
- ☐ 1h 89mins
- ☐ 2h 19mins
- ☐ 1h 19mins
- ☐ 1h 29mins

2. 4 hours and 30 minutes is equal to:
- ☐ 430 minutes
- ☐ 150 minutes
- ☐ 210 minutes
- ☐ 270 minutes

3. $2\frac{3}{4}$ hours is the same as:
- ☐ 234 minutes
- ☐ 2·75 hours
- ☐ 45 minutes
- ☐ 2 hours 34 minutes

4. The time on the alarm clock shows:

16:55
- ☐ 5 minutes to 5 in the morning
- ☐ 5 minutes past 5 in the evening
- ☐ 5 minutes past 5 in the morning
- ☐ 5 minutes to 5 in the evening

rough work

5. The time on the alarm clock shows:

17:35
- ☐ 25 to 8 in the evening
- ☐ 25 to 4 in the evening
- ☐ 25 to 7 in the morning
- ☐ 25 to 6 in the evening

6. 22:55 is the same as:
- ☐ 10:55am
- ☐ 5 to 2
- ☐ 10:55pm
- ☐ 5 past 2

7. How many minutes are there from 13:46 to 15:04?
- ☐ 2h 42mins
- ☐ 242mins
- ☐ 118mins
- ☐ 1h 18mins

8. If the news began at 17:55 and lasted for 45 minutes, at what time did it end?
- ☐ 18:00
- ☐ 20 to 7 in the evening
- ☐ 6:30 pm
- ☐ 20 to 7 in the morning

rough work

Topic 17: Percentages 1

A. Warm up!

Fill in the missing values.

1. 10% + 40% + ____ = 1
2. ____ + 35% + 15% = 1
3. 33% + ____ + 17% = 1
4. 11% + 29% + ____ = 1
5. 89% + ____ + 2% = 1
6. 74% + 6% + ____ = 1
7. 19% + 26% + 55% = ____
8. 15% + 46% + 39% = ____

B. In your mathematical opinion

1. There are **24** hours in a day. Yesterday, Alan spent **12** hours sleeping.
   What percentage was that? ____
2. Estimate and then find out what percentage of your day you spend eating, sleeping, at school, doing homework and watching television. You may use your calculator to help you. _____, _____, _____, _____, _____

C. Calculate!

1. Write each of these decimals as percentages.
   (a) 0·5 ____   (b) 0·25 ____   (c) 0·3 ____   (d) 0·75 ____   (e) 0·4 ____   (f) 0·8 ____

2. Write each of these fractions as percentages.
   (a) $\frac{1}{2}$ ____   (b) $\frac{1}{4}$ ____   (c) $\frac{3}{4}$ ____   (d) $\frac{1}{5}$ ____
   (e) $\frac{2}{3}$ ____   (f) $\frac{3}{5}$ ____   (g) $\frac{1}{10}$ ____   (h) $\frac{1}{20}$ ____

3. Write each of these percentages as decimals and fractions.
   (a) 80% ____, ____   (b) 25% ____, ____   (c) 30% ____, ____   (d) 20% ____, ____
   (e) 5% ____, ____   (f) 95% ____, ____   (g) 45% ____, ____   (h) 100% ____, ____

C. True or false?

1. $\frac{1}{2} > 55\%$ ☐ true ☐ false
2. $33\% = 0.3$ ☐ true ☐ false
3. $\frac{4}{5} = 80\%$ ☐ true ☐ false
4. $0.95 > 90\%$ ☐ true ☐ false
5. $1.1 = 100\%$ ☐ true ☐ false
6. $\frac{3}{4} > 80\%$ ☐ true ☐ false

D. Real life maths

Use the euro coins and notes to help you write 10 statements e.g. 5c is 5% of €1.

1. ___ is ___% of ___
2. ___ is ___% of ___
3. ___ is ___% of ___
4. ___ is ___% of ___
5. ___ is ___% of ___
6. ___ is ___% of ___
7. ___ is ___% of ___
8. ___ is ___% of ___
9. ___ is ___% of ___
10. ___ is ___% of ___

E. Word puzzles

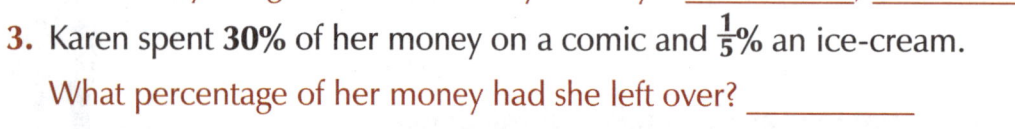

1. **0·25** of Áine's money is **€10.** How much is all her money? _____
2. **50%** of the children in 5th Class are girls. There are **36** children in the class. How many are girls and how many are boys? _____, _____
3. Karen spent **30%** of her money on a comic and $\frac{1}{5}$% an ice-cream. What percentage of her money had she left over? _____
4. **0·6** of the days in July had rain. What fraction of July had no rain? _____
5. Tom had **€90**. He spent **40%** of his money on a hurley. How much money had he left? _____
6. $\frac{1}{5}$ of the **30** children in 6th Class play chess. How many children do not play chess? _____

Test yourself!

1. 0·35 is equivalent to:
   - ☐ 0·35%
   - ☐ 35%
   - ☐ $3\frac{5}{100}$
   - ☐ $\frac{35}{1000}$

2. 75% is equivalent to:
   - ☐ 75·00
   - ☐ 0·075
   - ☐ 0·75
   - ☐ $7\frac{5}{100}$

3. $\frac{4}{5}$ is equivalent to:
   - ☐ $4\frac{5}{100}$
   - ☐ 45
   - ☐ 0·45
   - ☐ 80%

4. 0·25 of 36 is:
   - ☐ 61
   - ☐ 11
   - ☐ 35·75
   - ☐ 9

5. 60% of 70 is:
   - ☐ 130
   - ☐ 10
   - ☐ 7
   - ☐ 42

6. $\frac{1}{3}$ of a number is 5. The whole number is:
   - ☐ 8
   - ☐ 15
   - ☐ 35
   - ☐ 135

7. 0·45 of a number is 45. The whole number is:
   - ☐ 450
   - ☐ 90
   - ☐ 4.5
   - ☐ 100

8. 75% of a number is 12. The whole number is:
   - ☐ 16
   - ☐ 4
   - ☐ 9
   - ☐ 36

9. There were 300 people at a camogie match 0·4 were men, 20% were women and the rest were children. How many children were there?
   - ☐ 0·25 were children
   - ☐ 40 were children
   - ☐ $\frac{1}{3}$ were children
   - ☐ 120 were children

10. 280 trees were planted in a field. 40% were beech, 15% were oak and the rest were ash trees. Which statement describes how many trees of each specimen there were?
    - ☐ 40 beech; 15 oak; 45 ash
    - ☐ 112% beech; 42% oak; 126% ash
    - ☐ 0·112 beech; 0·42 oak; 0·126 ash
    - ☐ 112 beech; 42 oak; 126 ash

Topic 18 Money

A. Warm up!

Write these amounts using the € sign.

1. 9c ____
2. 15c ____
3. 28c ____
4. 124c ____
5. 200c ____
6. 1,010c ____
7. 2,550c ____
8. 30,000c ____
9. 45,000c ____
10. 55,550c ____

B. In your mathematical opinion

1. Can you estimate the cost of your lunch today? ____
2. For a sandwich, what is the cost of the slices of bread? ____
3. What is the cost of the butter or margarine? ____
4. Find the total cost of your lunch today and then calculate the total cost for 1 school year. ____

C. Calculate!

1. **Write these amounts using the cent sign.**

    (a) €0·07 ____ (b) €0·25 ____ (c) €0·94 ____ (d) €1·06 ____ (e) €1·33 ____
    (f) €5·66 ____ (g) €10·24 ____ (h) €129·32 ____ (i) €205·34 ____ (j) €524·08 ____

2. **Calculate.**

    (a) 50c + €2·36 + 8c = ____
    (b) €10·23 + 86c + €1·44 = ____
    (c) €26·78 + €1·49 + 12c + 4c = ____
    (d) €50 − €6·99 = ____
    (e) €11·38 − 99c = ____
    (f) (€100 − €49·99) + 76c = ____
    (g) (€50 + €12·99) − 99c = ____
    (i) (€0·99 + €2·49 + €20) − €6·49 = ____

3. **Calculate the cost for one of each of the following items.**

    (a) 6 oranges for €3·60. ____
    (b) 10 apples for €3·90 ____
    (c) 7 pears for €2·52 ____
    (d) 12 kiwis for €2·76 ____
    (e) 8 melons for €12·40 ____
    (f) 6 bananas for €2·88 ____

D. Operations

For each question say wheater you add, subtract, multiply or divide to find the answers.

1. What is the cost of five copies at 79c each? _____, _____
2. How much change would you have from €5 if you brought a bar of chocolate at 96c and a comic for €3·62? _____, _____
3. 10 pencils cost €5. How much for 15 of the same pencils? _____
4. 2 litres of sunflower oil costs €3·20.
   (a) How much for 1 litre? _____, _____
   (b) How much for 500ml? _____, _____

E. Real-life maths

Gillian's school tour is on the 22nd of June. From 1st January she saved 30c per day (it's not a leap year). The tour costs €35 and she would like to have €25 spending money.

1. Will Gillian have enough money saved by 22nd June? _____
2. On what date will she have the correct amount? _____
3. How long would it take Gillian to save €30? _____
4. How long would it take Gillian to save €120? _____

F. Word puzzles

1. Paula had €20. She bought a pencil case for €3·49 and some markers for €2·99. How much change had she from a €20 note? _____
2. Karla bought 25 tennis balls at 75c each. How much did they cost in total? _____
3. 3 melons cost €3·75. How much for one melon? _____
4. 2kg of potatoes cost €4·80. How much for 1·5kg? _____
5. 750ml of cream cost €2·10. How much for $\frac{1}{4}$ litre of cream? _____
6. Circle which is better value for money: (a) $\frac{1}{2}$kg of butter costs €2. $\frac{1}{4}$kg of butter costs 80c.
   (b) 2 metres of rope costs €6·64. 250cm of rope costs €1·20.
7. Cait bought 0·8kg of carrots for €1·40. Jackie bought $\frac{3}{5}$kg of carrots for €0·90. Who got the better deal and by how much? _____

Test yourself!

1. Write 60,483c using the € sign.
   - ☐ €60·483
   - ☐ €604·83
   - ☐ €6,048·30
   - ☐ €60,483

2. Write €1,263·41 using the c sign.
   - ☐ 12,634·1c
   - ☐ 1,263·41c
   - ☐ 126·341c
   - ☐ 126,341c

3. How many 5c in €2·40?
   - ☐ 28
   - ☐ 38
   - ☐ 48
   - ☐ 58

4. 2c is ___% of €1.
   - ☐ 2%
   - ☐ 20%
   - ☐ 0.2%
   - ☐ 0.02%

5. 5c is ___% of €10.
   - ☐ 1%
   - ☐ 5%
   - ☐ 0·5%
   - ☐ 50%

6. 6 tomatoes cost €1·80. How much for 8 tomatoes?
   - ☐ €1·88
   - ☐ €2·00
   - ☐ €2·40
   - ☐ €2·80

7. 9 red apples cost €5·40. How much for 6?
   - ☐ €4·80
   - ☐ €4·20
   - ☐ €4·00
   - ☐ €3·60

8. 1 metre of fence costs €6·60 to varnish. How much to varnish 0.75 metres?
   - ☐ €1·65
   - ☐ €5·85
   - ☐ €7·35
   - ☐ €4·95

9. $1\frac{1}{2}$ litres of milk costs €3·30. How much for $\frac{1}{4}$ litre?
   - ☐ €1·10
   - ☐ €2·20
   - ☐ €1·80
   - ☐ 55c

10. 0·25l of cranberry juice costs 85c. How much for $2\frac{1}{2}$ litres?
    - ☐ €3·40
    - ☐ €6·80
    - ☐ €8·50
    - ☐ €21·25

rough work

58 Planet Maths Activity Book • 5th Class

Topic 19: Percentages 2

A. Warm up!

Calculate these in your head.

1. 50% of 10 = ___
2. 25% of 12 = ___
3. 30% of 20 = ___
4. 70% of 70 = ___
5. 85% of 100 = ___
6. 90% of 200 = ___
7. 20% of 50 = ___
8. 25% of 28 = ___
9. 45% of 80 = ___

B. In your mathematical opinion

Estimate the percentage of the weekly shopping bill in your house that is spent on each of the following.

1. Fruit and vegetables _____
2. Meat _____
3. Dairy products (such as milk, eggs, cheese) _____
4. Cereals _____
5. Treats (such as bars and crisps) _____

C. Calculate!

1. **Calculate the whole number for each of these decimal fractions.**

   (a) 0·2 is 4 ____ (b) 0·1 is 10 ____ (c) 0·25 is 16 ____ (d) 0·5 is 25 ____
   (e) 0·3 is 40 ____ (f) 0·6 is 18 ____ (g) 0·4 is 12 ____ (h) 0·8 is 28 ____

2. **Calculate the whole number for each of these percentages.**

   (a) 20% is 22 ____ (b) 10% is 5 ____ (c) 25% is 8 ____ (d) 50% is 6 ____
   (e) 75% is 36 ____ (f) 40% is 32 ____ (g) 60% is 27 ____ (h) 5% is 10 ____

3. **Express the first number as a percentage of the second number.**

   (a) 2 and 10 ____ (b) 3 and 5 ____ (c) 1 and 4 ____ (d) 4 and 8 ____
   (e) 3 and 4 ____ (f) 4 and 5 ____ (g) 6 and 24 ____ (h) 5 and 25 ____

D. True or false?

1. $\frac{1}{2} > 0.45$ ☐ true ☐ false
2. $65\% < 0.7$ ☐ true ☐ false
3. $\frac{4}{5} > 80\%$ ☐ true ☐ false
4. 2 is 40% of 5 ☐ true ☐ false
5. $22\% < 0.23$ ☐ true ☐ false
6. $100\% > 1.1$ ☐ true ☐ false
7. $\frac{2}{3} = 75\%$ ☐ true ☐ false
8. $5\% > \frac{1}{20}$ ☐ true ☐ false

9. The X on the number line represents 80%. ☐ true ☐ false

   Number line marked: $\frac{1}{5}$, $\frac{2}{5}$, $\frac{3}{5}$, X, $\frac{4}{5}$

10. The X on the number line represents 75%. ☐ true ☐ false

    Number line marked: $\frac{1}{10}$, $\frac{2}{10}$, $\frac{3}{10}$, $\frac{4}{10}$, $\frac{5}{10}$, $\frac{6}{10}$, X, $\frac{8}{10}$, $\frac{9}{10}$

E. Real-life maths

Dave's electrical shop is having a sale. What is the new price of each of these items?

item	price	reduction	sale price
TV	€900	20%	
DVD player	€220	10%	
camera	€450	10%	
laptop computer	€1,000	25%	
printer	€120	5%	
scanner	€200	15%	

F. Word puzzles

1. **0·25** of Gareth's money is **€24**. How much is all his money? _____
2. **40%** of the children in 5th class cycle to school. **10** people cycle to school. How many are there in 5th Class altogether? _____
3. Sadhbh got **6** out of **10** in her spelling test. What percentage did she get? _____
4. A coat was **€80** before a sale. It was reduced by **10%**. What is the new price? _____
5. Kevin got **15** questions out of **20** correct in his test. What percentage did he get right? _____
6. **10** out of every **100** people in the United States have a passport. What percentage of people do not have a passport? _____

Test yourself!

1. 30% is equivalent to:
   - ☐ $\frac{3}{100}$
   - ☐ 0·03
   - ☐ 3·0
   - ☐ 0·3

2. 75% of a number is 9. The whole number is:
   - ☐ 69
   - ☐ 84
   - ☐ 3
   - ☐ 12

3. 20% of a number is 20. The whole number is:
   - ☐ 20
   - ☐ 0
   - ☐ 40
   - ☐ 100

4. What percentage of 100 is 25?
   - ☐ 100%
   - ☐ 25%
   - ☐ 4%
   - ☐ 75%

5. What percentage of 16 is 4?
   - ☐ 4%
   - ☐ 16%
   - ☐ 25%
   - ☐ 20%

6. Increase €75 by 20%.
   - ☐ €15
   - ☐ €95
   - ☐ €90
   - ☐ €77

7. Decrease €12 by 75%.
   - ☐ €3
   - ☐ €4
   - ☐ €63
   - ☐ €11·25

8. There were 25 children in a class, 10 of them are boys. What percentage are boys?
   - ☐ 10%
   - ☐ 40%
   - ☐ 25%
   - ☐ 15%

9. A farmer had 240 sheep. Another farmer had 100% more. How many sheep had the second farmer?
   - ☐ 140
   - ☐ 240
   - ☐ 300
   - ☐ 480

10. 100% of a number is 200. 110% of the number is:
    - ☐ 20
    - ☐ 210
    - ☐ 220
    - ☐ 330

Planet Maths Activity Book • 5th Class

TOPIC 20 Area

A. Warm up!

Estimate and then find the area of the following in centimetres squared (cm²).

1. This page ___
2. The lid of your lunchbox ___
3. Your teacher's desk ___

B. In your mathematical opinion

1. When you are standing up, how much area of the floor do you take up? ___
2. Can you estimate how many people, standing up, could fit in your classroom? ___

C. Calculate!

1. Find the area of each of the following shapes.

   (a) 8m × 2m

   (b) 8m × 8m

   (c) 10m, 8m, 20m, 4m

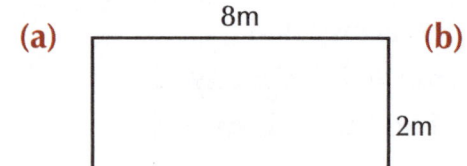

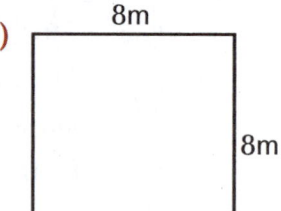

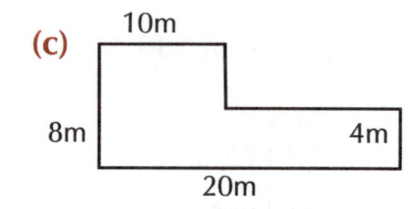

2. Fill in the table.

	length	width	perimeter	area
(a)	8cm	6cm		
(b)		7cm	28cm	49cm²
(c)	14cm		38cm	
(d)	5cm			25cm²
(e)		9cm		108cm²

3. Find the area and perimeter of each of these shapes.

   (a) 4m, 2m, 6m, 1m

   (b) 7m, 1m, 7m, 1m, 1m

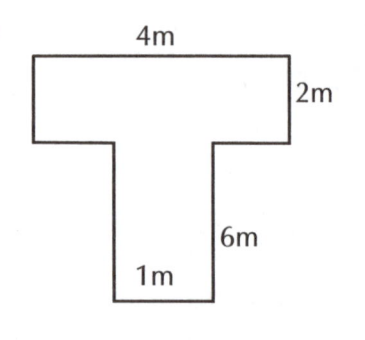

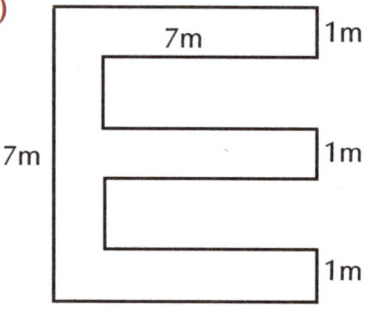

D. Real-life maths

1. What do these symbols mean in the floor plan below?

   _____   _____

2. What is the length of these rooms? Measure them at the longest point.

   (a) bathroom _____   (b) kitchen _____   (c) sitting room _____   (d) master bedroom _____

3. Which is the widest room in the house? _____

4. How much wider is the entrance hall than the wardrobe? _____

5. At the longest point, what length is the house? _____

6. If Joe wanted to put a trellis along the right side of the house, how much trellis would he need to buy? Don't cover the windows or doors! _____

7. If Joe walked from the couch in the sitting room, through the entrance hall, to the bed in bedroom 2, how far would he have walked?

Floor Plan Scale: 1cm is 1m

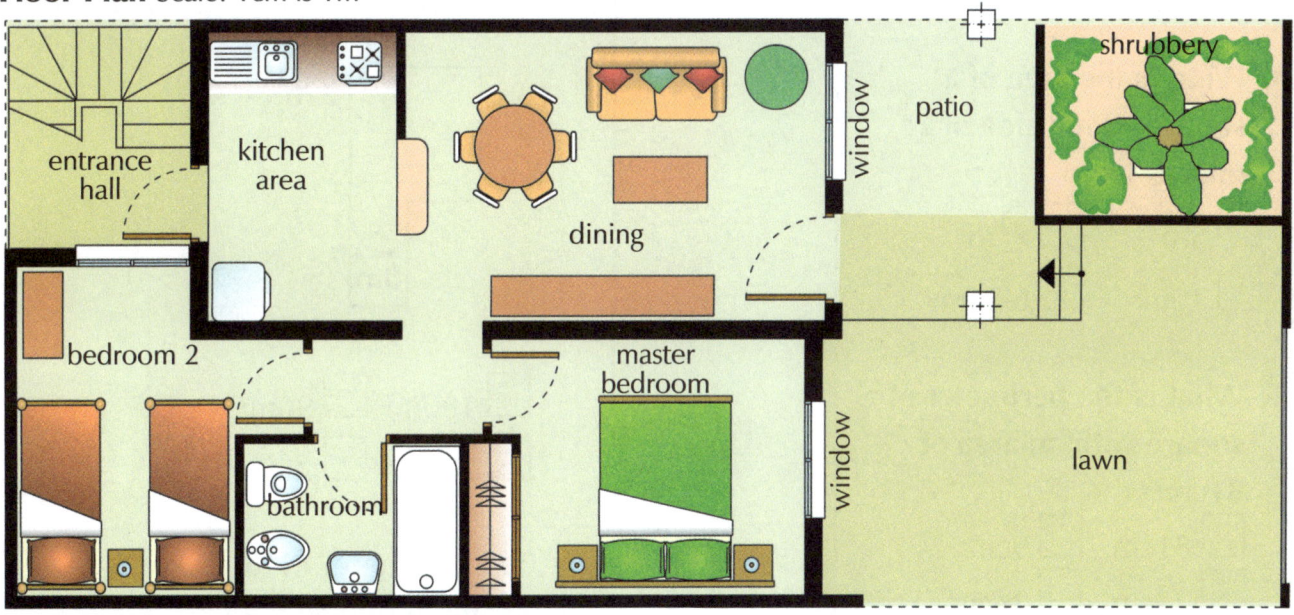

E. Word puzzles

1. An envelope is **15cm** long and **8cm** wide. What is its area? _____

2. A table mat has a length of **12cm** and a width of **10$\frac{1}{2}$cm**. What is its area? _____

3. The perimeter of a square garden is **36cm**. What is the length of a side? _____

4. The perimeter of a tennis court is **72 metres**. The length of a side is **28m**. What is its width? _____

Test yourself!

1. What is the area of this rectangle?

   13cm
   4cm

   ☐ 17cm² ☐ 21cm²
   ☐ 30cm² ☐ 34cm²

2. What is the area of a rectangle with a perimeter of 50 metres and a length of 17 metres?

   ☐ 136m² ☐ 67m²
   ☐ 36m² ☐ 8m²

3. What is the area of a square with a side of $2\frac{1}{2}$ metres is?

   ☐ 5m² ☐ $7\frac{1}{2}$m²
   ☐ 10m² ☐ 6·25m²

4. What is the perimeter of a square with an area of 81cm²?

   ☐ 81cm ☐ 9cm
   ☐ 27cm ☐ 36cm

5. The perimeter of a rectangular yard is 140m. The width of the yard is 25m. What is the area?

   ☐ 90m² ☐ 50m²
   ☐ 45m² ☐ 1,125m²

6. Flooring costs €21 per square metre. What is the cost of putting a floor down in this room?

   6m
   6m

   ☐ €12 ☐ €36
   ☐ €756 ☐ €57

7. The area of this shape is:

   18m
   10m   22m
   8m

   ☐ 180m² ☐ 96m²
   ☐ 276sm² ☐ 356m²

8. The perimeter of the shape in question 7 is:

   ☐ 276m ☐ 58m
   ☐ 78m ☐ 80m

Topic 21: Directed Numbers

A. Warm up!

Fill in the missing values on the number line.

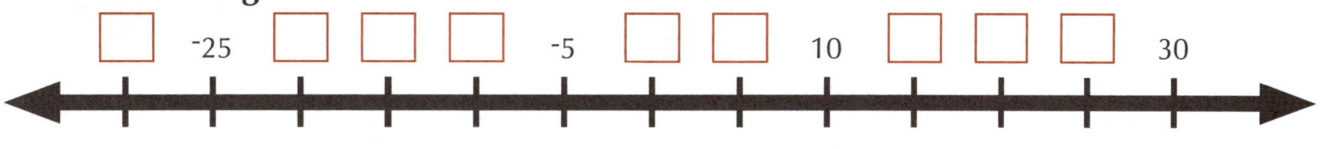

☐ -25 ☐ ☐ ☐ -5 ☐ ☐ 10 ☐ ☐ ☐ 30

B. In your mathematical opinion

Sheila works on a fifth floor of an office block. Her car is parked two stories under the ground. Sheila leaves the building for her lunch hour every day, but she does not use her car. **How many days would Sheila need to work to travel 1,000 floors?** _____

7
6
5 Sheila's Floor
4
3
2
1
0 Ground Floor
-1
-2

C. Calculate!

1. **What is the difference between each of these pairs?**

    (a) $^-5$ and $^+2$ ___   (b) $^-8$ and $^+1$ ___   (c) $^-2$ and $^+2$ ___
    (d) $^-2$ and $^+12$ ___   (e) $^-1$ and $^+3$ ___   (f) $^-11$ and $^+9$ ___
    (g) $^-4$ and $^+15$ ___   (h) $^-14$ and $^+6$ ___   (i) $^-20$ and $^+8$ ___

2. **Circle the city in each pair that has the colder temperature. By how many degrees?**

    (a) Dublin $^+11$ °C & London $^+14$ °C _____   (b) Glasgow $^+8$ °C & Amsterdam $^+4$ °C _____
    (c) Chicago $^-1$ °C & LA $^+18$ °C _____   (d) Helsinki $^+2$ °C & St Petersburg $^-4$ °C _____
    (e) Oslo $^-10$ °C & Stockholm $^-13$ °C _____   (f) Tokyo $^+12$ °C & Hong Kong $^+26$ °C _____
    (g) Reykjavik $^-22$ °C & Toronto $^-14$ °C _____ (h) Perth $^+32$ °C & Prague $^-2$ °C _____
    (i) Cork $^+16$ °C & Budapest $^-6$ °C _____   (j) Prague 0 °C & Madrid $^+29$ °C _____

Based on Planet Maths 5 page 133, 134, 135, 136 and 137

D. True or false?

The bar line chart shows how much money each person has in their savings account at the Credit Union. Read the bar chart and answer true or false.

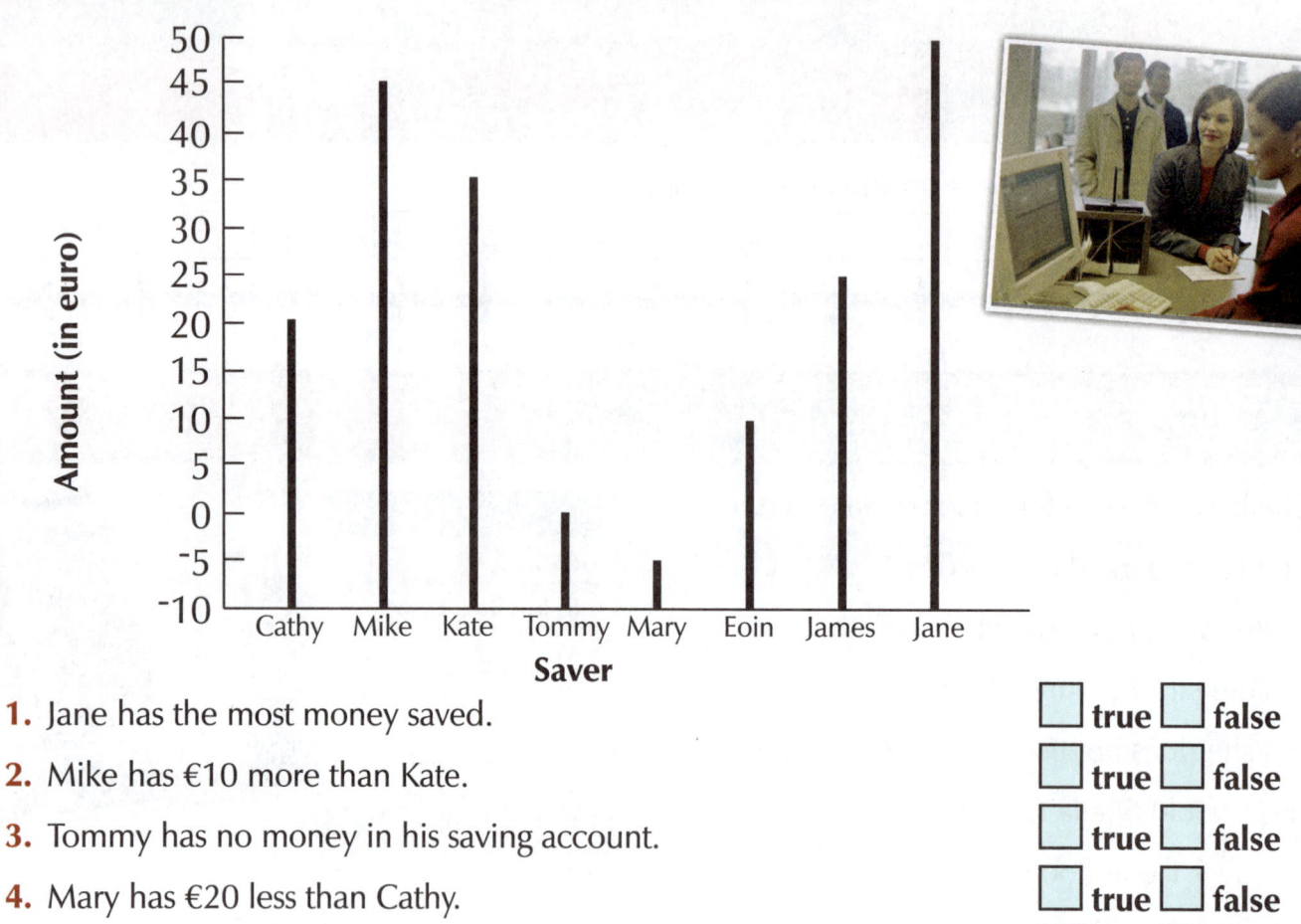

1. Jane has the most money saved. ☐ true ☐ false
2. Mike has €10 more than Kate. ☐ true ☐ false
3. Tommy has no money in his saving account. ☐ true ☐ false
4. Mary has €20 less than Cathy. ☐ true ☐ false
5. Mike, Eoin and Jane have €70 altogether. ☐ true ☐ false
6. The difference between Tommy and Mary's amounts is €5. ☐ true ☐ false

E. Word Puzzles

1. Justin went from 2 levels underground to 7 levels above ground in a hotel lift. How many floors did he travel? _____
2. A video counter shows ⁻13 minutes. How many minutes are there till it shows ⁺26 minutes? _____
3. A golfer had a score if ⁻2 on Saturday. His partner had a score of ⁺8. Who had the best score and by how many points? _____
4. The temperature of the water in the tap is ⁺4ºC. The temperature of an ice cube is ⁻3ºC. Which is warmer and by how many degrees? _____

Test yourself!

1. What is the difference between -4 and +1?
   - ☐ +5
   - ☐ -5
   - ☐ +3
   - ☐ -3

2. What is the difference between 0 and -12?
   - ☐ +12
   - ☐ -12
   - ☐ 0
   - ☐ none of the above

3. It is +33°C in Seville and -2°C in Moscow. Which city is warmer and by how many degrees?
   - ☐ Seville by +31°C
   - ☐ Moscow by +31°C
   - ☐ Moscow by +35°C
   - ☐ Seville by +35°C

4. What is the difference in temperature between Helsinki at -10°C and Darwin at +38°C?
   - ☐ +10 °C
   - ☐ +38 °C
   - ☐ +28 °C
   - ☐ +48 °C

5. A video counter shows -32 minutes. How long will it be until it shows +12 minutes?
   - ☐ 20 mins
   - ☐ 12 mins
   - ☐ 32 mins
   - ☐ 44 mins

rough work

6. Bob has -4 points and Martin has +5 points. Who has more points and by how many?
   - ☐ Bob by +4 points
   - ☐ Martin by +5 points
   - ☐ Martin by +9 points
   - ☐ Bob by +1 points

7. Deirdre has €100 in the bank. If she withdraws €120 what is her balance?
   - ☐ +€220
   - ☐ +€20
   - ☐ -€20
   - ☐ -€220

8. Fergus has €75 in the bank. Alan owes the bank €25. How much more money has Fergus?
   - ☐ +€100
   - ☐ +€50
   - ☐ +€90
   - ☐ +€25

9. What number is halfway between -5 and +5?
   - ☐ 0
   - ☐ +1
   - ☐ -1
   - ☐ +2

10. What number is halfway between -10 and +4?
    - ☐ -3
    - ☐ -2
    - ☐ -1

rough work

Topic 22 — The Circle

A. Warm up!

Name the following shapes.

1. 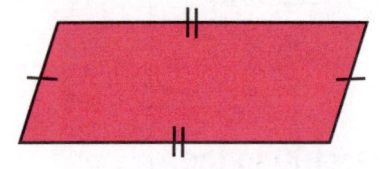 _____
2. 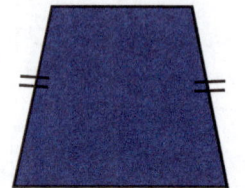 _____
3. 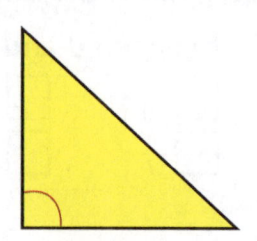 _____
4. 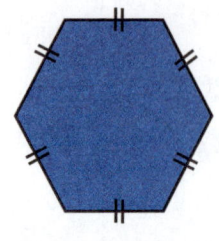 _____
5. 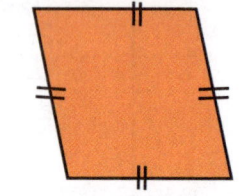 _____
6. _____

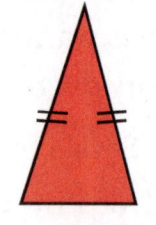

B. In your mathematical opinion

How many €1 coins laid end-to-end would be the length of your body?

How will you estimate? _____

C. Fill in the missing words

1. The _____ is the line from the centre of a circle to its edge.
2. The _____ is the name of the curved edge of a circle.
3. A line that goes from one edge of the circle to another through the centre point is called the _____.
4. A line that goes from one point of the edge of a circle to another without going through the centre point is called _____.
5. The area between two radii is called a _____.
6. _____ is the name for the part of the circumference between two radii.

D. Real-life maths

This is a plan of a garden. What is the length and width of the garden if each of the circles are the same size and the length of the radius is 6 metres?

Length: _____   Width: _____

E. Word puzzles

1. The area of a semi-circle is **24m²** squared. What is the area of the whole circle? _____
2. If the radius of a bicycle wheel is **30cm**, what is its diameter? _____
3. The perimeter of the following garden is **30 metres**. What is the length of the circumference of the semi-circle? _____

   8m
   8m
   8m

4. In the garden above, the area of the square part is double the area of the semi-circle. What is the area of the garden? _____
5. The diameter of a 2 cent coin is approximately **8mm**. What is the length of ten 2 cent coins laid end-to-end? _____

F. Puzzle

How many €2 coins would you need to reach your height if the coins were stacked end to end? _____
(The diameter of a €2 coin is 25mm.)

Test yourself!

1. What is marked on this diagram at A?

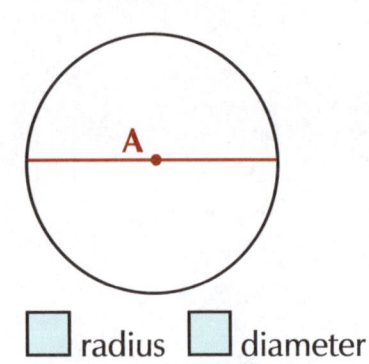

   ☐ radius ☐ diameter
   ☐ chord   ☐ arc

2. What is the name of the curved line marked A?

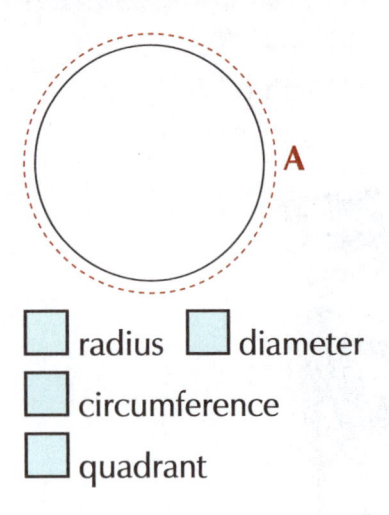

   ☐ radius   ☐ diameter
   ☐ circumference
   ☐ quadrant

3. What is marked on this diagram?

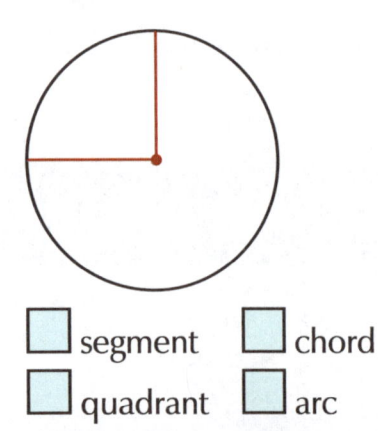

   ☐ segment   ☐ chord
   ☐ quadrant ☐ arc

4. The diameter of a circle is 14cm. The radius is:
   ☐ 14cm   ☐ 21cm
   ☐ 7cm   ☐ 12cm

5. The radius of a circle is 90mm. The diameter is:
   ☐ 9cm   ☐ 45mm
   ☐ 18cm   ☐ 18mm

6. The area between the chord of a circle and the circumference is called the:
   ☐ segment
   ☐ arc
   ☐ sector
   ☐ semi-circle

7. The quadrant of a circle is exactly what fraction of a circle?
   ☐ $\frac{1}{2}$ ☐ $\frac{1}{3}$
   ☐ $\frac{1}{4}$ ☐ $\frac{1}{5}$

8. How many degrees are there in a circle?
   ☐ 300°   ☐ 400°
   ☐ 360°   ☐ 460°

Topic 23: Rules and Properties

A. Warm up!

Draw the next three terms in the following sequence.

1. ■ ● ▲ ◆ ●
2. X Y Z 1 X Y Z 2 ___ ___ ___
3. ✻ ! [ ] € ✻ ! [ ] ___ ___ ___
4. 🌳 ☀️ ⛈️ ☁️ 🌳 ☀️ ___ ___ ___ ___

B. In your mathematical opinion

1. Pick any numbers between 1 and 9 and use them in the following calculation.

    (___ + ___) x (___ x ___) = ___

2. How many different answers can you get by moving the numbers above around? ___

C. Calculate!

1. Write the next three terms in each sequence.

    (a) 42, 45, 48, 51, ___, ___, ___
    (b) 470, 490, 510, 530 ___, ___, ___
    (c) 1, 4, 16, 64, ___, ___, ___
    (d) 98, 91, 84 ___, ___, ___
    (e) 115·5, 105·5, 95·5, ___, ___, ___
    (f) 1, 2, 4, 7, 11, ___, ___, ___
    (g) 5, 30, 180, ___, ___, ___
    (h) $2\frac{1}{4}$, $2\frac{1}{2}$, $2\frac{3}{4}$, ___, ___, ___
    (i) $3\frac{1}{8}$, $2\frac{7}{8}$, $2\frac{5}{8}$, ___, ___, ___
    (j) $1\frac{3}{10}$, $1\frac{1}{5}$, $1\frac{1}{10}$, ___, ___, ___

2. What are the missing terms in each sequence?

    (a) 2, 4, ___, ___, 10
    (b) 14, ___, 28, ___, 42
    (c) ___, 45, ___, 27, 18
    (d) ___, ___, 110, 105, 10
    (e) 40, ___, ___, 160, 200
    (f) 72, 81, 90, ___, ___
    (g) 11, ___, 44, ___, 176
    (h) $\frac{1}{2}$, $\frac{3}{4}$, ___, $1\frac{1}{4}$, $1\frac{1}{2}$, ___

D. True or false?

Remember the rule: My Dear Aunt Sally.

1. 6 + 4 ÷ 4 = 2·5
2. 12 − 54 ÷ 9 = 6
3. (4 x 2) + 23 = 100
4. (9 ÷ 3) x 6 = 18
5. 24 ÷ (12 ÷ 3) = 6
6. 12 x 8 + (108 ÷ 12) = 17
7. (1·25 x 10) − 10 = 1·25
8. (6·5 ÷ 5) x 10 = 13
9. 16 x 14 − 200 = 24
10. 24 − (36 ÷ 9) = 1·3

☐ true ☐ false (×10)

E. Real-life maths

1,000 raffle tickets were sold at Scoil Ciaran's Nativity Play. They were numbered from 1 to 1,000.

1. (a) How many tickets have one 9? _____
   (b) What is the highest numeber with one 9? _____
2. (a) How many tickets have two 9s? _____
   (b) What is the highest number with two 9s? _____
3. How many tickets have three 9s? _____

F. Numbr puzzles

What is the pattern? The first one has been done with you.

1. 5, 10, 15, 20, 25 **Add 5**
2. 2, 3, 5, 7, 11 _____
3. 6, 12, 18, 24, 30 _____
4. 1, 4, 9, 16, 25 _____
5. 152, 140, 128, 116, 104 _____
6. 1, 2, 3, 4, 6, 12 _____
7. 21, 22, 24, 25, 26, 27, 28, 30 _____
8. 1, 2, 4, 7, 14, 28 _____
9. 9, 18, 27, 36, 45 _____
10. 2·5, 3·1, 3·7, 4·3, 4·9, 5·5 _____

Test yourself!

1. What are the next three terms in this sequence?
   141, 131, 122, 114
   ☐ 106, 99, 93
   ☐ 107, 101, 96
   ☐ 105, 97, 90
   ☐ 104, 95, 87

2. Which is the odd one out in this sequence?
   2, 3, 5, 7, 11, 15
   ☐ 5   ☐ 7
   ☐ 11   ☐ 15

3. What is the rule for this sequence?
   16, 25, 36, 49, 64
   ☐ add 9
   ☐ add 11
   ☐ square numbers
   ☐ rectangular numbers

4. What is the rule for this sequence?
   1, 3, 7, 21
   ☐ multiples of 21
   ☐ factors of 7
   ☐ factors of 21
   ☐ multiples of 3

5. Which is the odd one out in this sequence?
   $\frac{1}{8}, \frac{1}{4}, \frac{3}{8}, \frac{1}{2}, \frac{5}{8}, \frac{3}{4}$
   ☐ $\frac{1}{8}$ ☐ $\frac{3}{8}$
   ☐ $\frac{5}{6}$ ☐ $\frac{3}{4}$

6. $144 \div (8 \times 2) = $ _____
   ☐ 14·25   ☐ 9
   ☐ 18   ☐ 36

7. $50 - 75 \div 5 = $ _____
   ☐ 35   ☐ 5
   ☐ ⁻25   ☐ 15

8. $(19 \times 8) - 8 = $ _____
   ☐ 19   ☐ 144
   ☐ 0   ☐ 152

9. What is the missing operator? $+, -, \times$ or $\div$
   19 ____ 8 ÷ 10 = 15·2
   ☐ +   ☐ −
   ☐ ×   ☐ ÷

10. What is the missing operator? _____
    (11·3 × 5) ____ 56 = 0·5
    ☐ +   ☐ −
    ☐ ×   ☐ ÷

Topic 24 — Weight

A. Warm up!

What weight is shown on each of these scales?

1. _____   2. _____   3. _____   4. _____

B. In your mathematical opinion

1. Ciara takes one teaspoon of sugar in her tea. How many grams of sugar does a teaspoon hold? ___

2. Ciara has two cups of tea every day.
   (a) How much sugar does she have in her tea every week? ___
   (b) How much sugar does she have in her tea in 30 days? ___
   (c) How many days will it take Ciara to use 1kg of sugar? ___

C. Calculate!

1. Write each of these weights as kilograms and grams.
   (a) 2,300g ___   (b) 1,785g ___   (c) 1,150g ___   (d) 5,005g ___
   (e) 4,050g ___   (f) $1\frac{1}{2}$kg ___   (g) $2\frac{1}{4}$kg ___   (h) $1\frac{3}{10}$kg ___

2. Write each of these weights as kilograms using the decimal point.
   (a) 1,400g ___   (b) 850g ___   (c) 2,040g ___   (d) 3,009g ___
   (e) 60g ___   (f) $1\frac{1}{5}$g ___   (g) $2\frac{3}{4}$kg ___   (h) $3\frac{9}{10}$kg ___

D. True or false?

1. 1·2 kg = 1,200g □ true □ false
2. 0·08 kg = 800g □ true □ false
3. $1\frac{2}{5}$ kg = 1,400g □ true □ false
4. 1,100g > 1·1 kg □ true □ false
5. 2kg 30g = 2·03kg □ true □ false
6. 4,500g < $4\frac{3}{4}$kg □ true □ false
7. 6g > 0·005kg □ true □ false
8. 3,080g = 3·8kg □ true □ false
9. $\frac{11}{1000}$ kg = 0·011kg □ true □ false
10. 210g = $\frac{21}{1000}$ kg □ true □ false

E. Real life maths

How long will a 10kg bag of potatoes last this family? They have potatoes with their dinner 5 times a week. _____

	Mr O'Shea	Mrs O'Shea	Jack	Maria	Edward
amount of potatoes with each dinner	720g	0·5kg	$\frac{4}{10}$kg	300g	$\frac{1}{4}$kg

F. Word puzzles

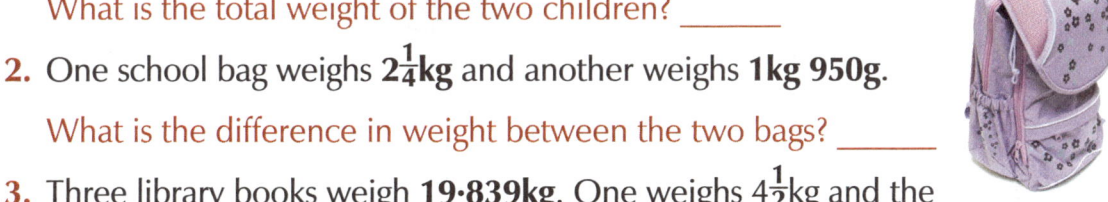

1. Jim weighs **45·6kg** and Caroline weighs **$40\frac{4}{5}$kg**. What is the total weight of the two children? _____
2. One school bag weighs **$2\frac{1}{4}$kg** and another weighs **1kg 950g**. What is the difference in weight between the two bags? _____
3. Three library books weigh **19·839kg**. One weighs **$4\frac{1}{2}$kg** and the second weighs **$6\frac{9}{10}$kg**. What is the weight of the third? _____
4. An envelope weighs **0·001kg**. What is the weight of 50 such envelopes? Give your answer in grams. _____ 
5. **250g** of meat costs **€2·40**. How much is it for 1kg of meat? _____
6. A jar of sweets of weighs **$1\frac{1}{2}$kg**. How many 30g bags of sweets can be filled from this jar? _____ 
7. Tea costs **€2·44** per quarter kilogram. How much would **$1\frac{1}{3}$kg** of tea cost? _____
8. How many buckets of coal each weighing **8·75kg** can be taken from a bag of coal weighing **175kg**? _____

Test yourself!

1. 1·05kg written as grams is:
   - ☐ 1,500g
   - ☐ 105g
   - ☐ 1,050g
   - ☐ 1,005g

2. 1,600g is equivalent to:
   - ☐ 1·06kg
   - ☐ $1\frac{3}{5}$kg
   - ☐ 106kg
   - ☐ $1\frac{6}{100}$kg

3. $4\frac{3}{4}$kg is equivalent to:
   - ☐ 4,340g
   - ☐ 4,430g
   - ☐ 475g
   - ☐ 4,750g

4. How many grams in $2\frac{1}{10}$ kg?
   - ☐ 210g
   - ☐ 2,010g
   - ☐ 2,100g
   - ☐ 2,110g

5. How much less than 2kg is 1·75kg?
   - ☐ 25g
   - ☐ 25kg
   - ☐ 150g
   - ☐ $\frac{1}{4}$kg

6. What is the approx. weight of the carrots?
   - ☐ 200g
   - ☐ 150g
   - ☐ 300g
   - ☐ 100g

rough work

7. How many bowls of sugar weighing 0·2kg can be made from a bag of sugar weighing 1·4kg?
   - ☐ 6
   - ☐ 7
   - ☐ 14
   - ☐ 2

8. What is the cost of $\frac{1}{4}$kg of meat if 2kg is €6·80?
   - ☐ €3·40
   - ☐ €1·70
   - ☐ €2
   - ☐ €0·85

9. What is the cost of $\frac{3}{4}$kg of jam if 1kg is €2?
   - ☐ 75c
   - ☐ €1
   - ☐ €1·75
   - ☐ €1·50

10. How much change would you have from €10 if 450g of fish costs €1·68 and you bought 2·25kg?
    - ☐ €8·40
    - ☐ €1·60
    - ☐ €3·78
    - ☐ €6·22

rough work

Topic 25: Number Sentences

A. Warm up!

Write true or false after each of these number sentences.

1. 16 x 8 = 108 _____
2. 112 = (10 x 12) – 8 _____
3. 183 > (20 + 5) x 8 _____
4. 153 ÷ 9 = 15 + 2 _____
5. (22 x 8) + 11 < 176 _____
6. 174 ÷ 3 = 50 + 1 _____
7. 9 + 4 x 2 = 17 _____
8. $\frac{1}{2}$ of 72 = 9 x 4 _____
9. 20 + 2 = $\frac{1}{4}$ of 96 _____
10. 22 x 22 = (11 x 2) x 22 _____

B. Calculate!

1. **Fill in the correct mathematical sign, < + – x ÷ >, to make each of these number sentences true.**

   (a) 8 ___ 7 = 56
   (b) (100 ___ 20) + 1 = 6
   (c) 17 ___ 9 = 155 – 2
   (d) 234 ___ 13 = 6 x 3
   (e) 199 ___ (24 x 6) x 7
   (f) 211 ___ 220 – 10
   (g) 11 ___ 6 ___ 5 = 11 x 2
   (h) (14 ___ 8) ___ 5 = 11

2. **Write the correct number to make each of these mathematical sentences true.**

   (a) ___ ÷ 10 = 20
   (b) 16 x ___ = 400
   (c) (13 + ___) – 8 = 42
   (d) ___ ÷ 13 = 16
   (e) (___ x 9) + 4 = 76
   (f) 150 = (___ x 4) + 22
   (g) (342 ÷ ___) = 20 – 1
   (h) (11 x ___) + 8 = 20 x 7

3. **Solve the equations.**

   (a) $\frac{1}{4}$ of 64 = ___
   (b) $\frac{3}{8}$ of 24 = ___
   (c) $\frac{4}{9}$ of 108 = ___
   (d) 10% of 50 = ___
   (e) 25% of 75 = ___
   (f) 0·7 of 30 = ___
   (g) 0·75 of 32 = ___
   (h) 0·09 of 200 = ___

D. True or false?

1. **A number multiplied by three is twenty-seven.**
   The unknown number is twenty-one. ☐ true ☐ false

2. **Fifteen multiplied by a number is sixty.**
   The unknown number is four. ☐ true ☐ false

3. **A number subtracted by fifteen is thirty-eight.**
   The unknown number is twenty-three. ☐ true ☐ false

4. **One-hundred and nine added to a number is two-hundred and eleven.**
   The unknown number is three hundred and twenty. ☐ true ☐ false

5. **Fifty per cent of a number is thirty.**
   The unknown number is sixty. ☐ true ☐ false

6. **Three-quarters of a number is twenty-four.**
   The unknown number is eighteen. ☐ true ☐ false

E. Real-life maths

Each of these children has savings with the Credit Union.

Jack	Ciara	David	Mikhail	Karen	Eleanor
€60	€119	€100	€130	€30	€120

In your of copy, write at least five word and number sentences using the amounts above.

For example, Jack has half the amount of money that Eleanor has, €60 = $\frac{1}{2}$ of €120.

F. Word puzzles

1. Tomas scored **sixty-four** points in a game of Scrabble. Carole scored **thirteen** points more. How many points had Carole? _____
2. A volleyball team of **six** players each had **three** jerseys. How many jerseys in total did the team have? _____
3. There are **twenty-four** children in 5th class. Half of them go to tin whistle lessons. How many take lessons? _____

Test yourself!

1. What is the missing mathematical sign?

   29 __ 6 = 40 − 5

   ☐ +   ☐ −
   ☐ ×   ☐ ÷

2. What is the missing mathematical sign?

   (135 __ 5) + 3 = 30

   ☐ +   ☐ −
   ☐ ×   ☐ ÷

3. What is the missing number?

   __ ÷ 6 + 9 = 18

   ☐ 2   ☐ 54
   ☐ 72   ☐ 33

4. What is the missing number?

   (8 × __) − 6 = 50 × 5

   ☐ 4   ☐ 24
   ☐ 32   ☐ 88

5. The sum 'thirty-six and seven is forty-one' as an equation is:

   ☐ 41 = 36 + 7
   ☐ 36 + 7 + 41 = 82
   ☐ 41 − 36 = 7
   ☐ 36 = 41 − 7

6. Eight made nine times greater is seventy-two. As an equation this is:

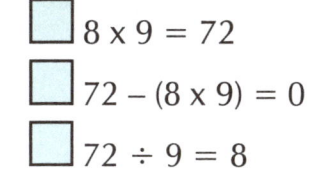

   ☐ 576 ÷ 8 = 72
   ☐ 8 × 9 = 72
   ☐ 72 − (8 × 9) = 0
   ☐ 72 ÷ 9 = 8

7. Sixty-nine minus a number is forty-six. As a equation this is:

   ☐ 69 × 46 = ___
   ☐ ___ = 69 + 46
   ☐ 69 − ___ = 46
   ☐ 69 − 46 = ___

8. A T-shirt costs €13. A jacket cost three times that amount. The correct number sentence for this is:

   ☐ €13 ÷ 3 = ___
   ☐ €13 − €3 = ___
   ☐ €13 + €3 = ___
   ☐ €13 × 3 = ___

rough work

rough work

Topic 26: 3D Shapes

A. Warm up!

Name each of these 3D shapes.

1. 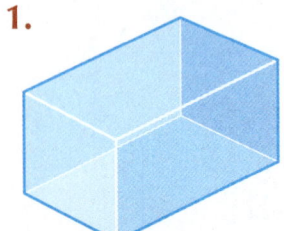
2. 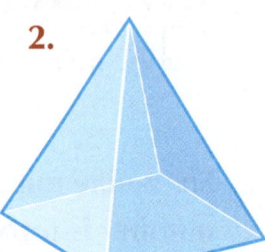
3. 
4.

B. In your mathematical opinion

You will need an A4 piece of paper. Write your answers in your copy.

1. Make a regular octagon by making six folds in the paper. How will you do this?
2. Is it possible to make an octagon using less than six folds? How?

C. Calculate!

Fill in the table.

	name	number of faces	2D shape of each face	number of vertices	number of edges
1. 					
2. 					
3.					
4. 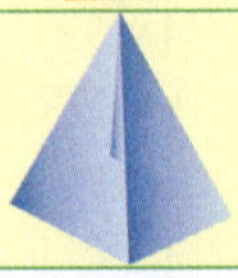					

D. Fill in the missing words

1. A cube has _____ faces, _____ vertices and _____ edges.
2. A cylinder has _____ faces, _____ vertices and _____ edges.
3. A cone has _____ faces, _____ vertices and _____ edges.
4. A hemisphere has _____ faces, _____ vertices and _____ edges.
5. A triangular prism has _____ faces, _____ vertices and _____ edges.
6. A tetrahedron has _____ faces, _____ vertices and _____ edges.
7. A cuboid has _____ faces, _____ vertices and _____ edges.
8. A rectangular-based pyramid has _____ faces, _____ vertices and _____ edges.

E. Real-life maths

Brian works for a paper and packaging company. He has to design a box. He must be able to stack the boxes so as to leave as little empty space as possible.

1. What kind of box should Brian design? _____
2. How many faces will it have? What 2D shape will each face be? How many edges and vertices will it have? _____, _____, _____
3. Sketch the net of the box Brian should make or construct it using whatever materials you have available in your classroom.

F. Puzzle

What shape is it?	shape A	shape B	shape C
It has:	5 faces	5 faces	6 faces
Its faces are:	square/triangle	triangles/rectangle	square
It has:	8 edges	9 edges	12 edges
It has:	5 vertices	6 vertices	8 vertices
It is a:			

Test yourself!

1. This shape is a:

   ☐ triangular prism
   ☐ equilateral triangle
   ☐ tetrahedron
   ☐ hexagonal pyramid

2. This shape is a:

   ☐ tetrahedron
   ☐ pentagon
   ☐ pentagonal pyramid
   ☐ pentagonal prism

3. How many faces has a cuboid?

   ☐ 4   ☐ 6
   ☐ 8   ☐ 10

4. How many edges has a triangular prism?

   ☐ 5   ☐ 6
   ☐ 7   ☐ 8

5. How many edges has a square pyramid?

   ☐ 5   ☐ 6
   ☐ 7   ☐ 8

6. This shape is a:

   ☐ hexagonal prism
   ☐ regular pyramid
   ☐ irregular pyramid
   ☐ irregular prism

7. This is the net of which shape?

   ☐ cylinder
   ☐ hemisphere
   ☐ isosceles triangle
   ☐ cone

8. This is the net of which shape?

   ☐ triangle
   ☐ pyramid
   ☐ tetrahedron
   ☐ triangular prism

Rough Work

Topic 27: Data 2

A. Warm up!

Find the average of each of the following sets.

1. 2, 4, 3 ____
2. 8, 9, 10 ____
3. 12, 19, 10, 3 ____
4. 20, 25, 22, 21 ____
5. €1·27, €2·50, €3, €3·79 ____
6. 100, 125, 130, 140, 145 ____
7. €200, €210, €300, €350, €400 ____
8. 14·5 °C, 22 °C, 25·5 °C, 27·5 °C, 29 °C ____

B. In your mathematical opinion

1. What is the average length of time spent doing homework in your class? How can you find out? _____
2. In your copy, design and draw a graph to show how much time any 10 people in your class spend on homework. Show the average on your graph using a broken line.

C. Calculate!

This pie chart shows the types of takeaway meals prefered by 12 people.

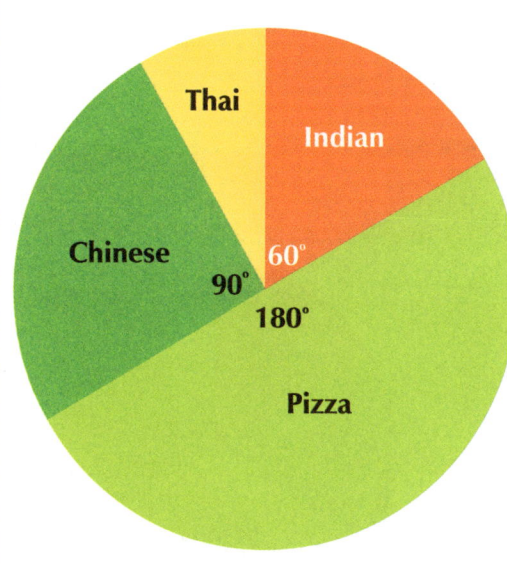

Thai
Indian 60°
Chinese 90°
Pizza 180°

1. How many people prefer pizza? _____
2. How many prefer Indian food? _____
3. What fraction prefer Chinese food? _____
4. What percentage prefer either Chinese food or pizza? _____
5. Twice as many people prefer Indian food to _____ food.

D. True or false?

This pie chart shows favourite sports as voted for by 100 people.

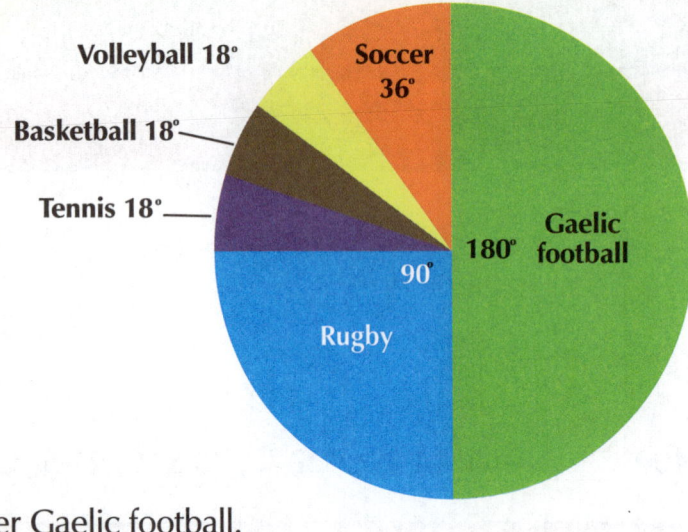

1. 50% prefer Gaelic football. ☐ true ☐ false
2. $\frac{1}{4}$ prefer rugby. ☐ true ☐ false
4. 5% prefer basketball. ☐ true ☐ false
5. 4 people prefer either basketball or tennis. ☐ true ☐ false

E. Real-life maths

A group of 16 students voted on their favourite holiday.

1. Show the information on the pie chart.

    America: 2   Spain: 8

    Portugal: 4   UK: 2

2. What fraction of children voted for the UK? _____
3. What percentage of children voted for Portugal? _____

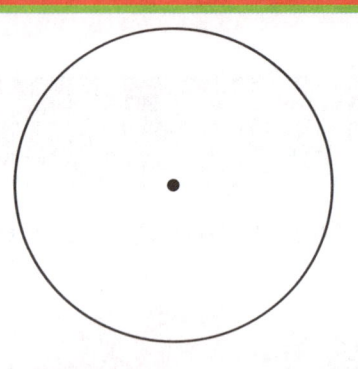

F. Puzzle

How the teachers at Colaiste Eanna come to school

6 teachers come to school by bicycle. What number of teachers use each of the other three modes of transport?

drive: _____   bus: _____   walk: _____

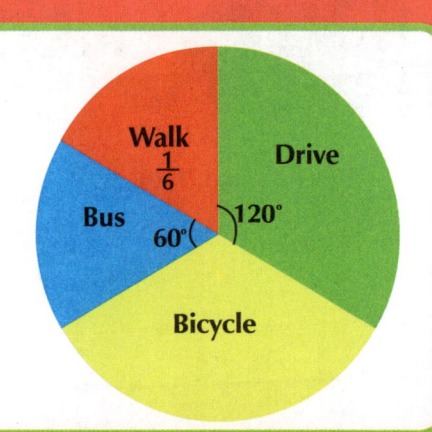

84 Planet Maths Activity Book • 5th Class

Test yourself!

1. The average of 82, 90 and 95 is:
   - ☐ 82
   - ☐ 267
   - ☐ 89
   - ☐ 90

2. Favourite zoo animal

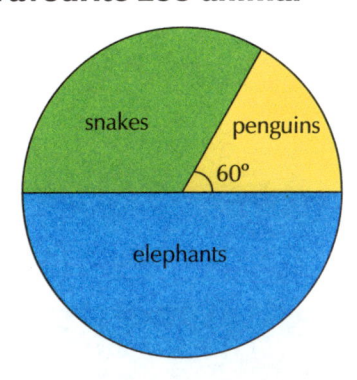

   (pie chart: snakes, penguins 60°, elephants)

   12 students voted for their favourite animal at the zoo. What percentage of children voted for the elephants?
   - ☐ 30%
   - ☐ 40%
   - ☐ 50%
   - ☐ 60%

3. What fraction of children in question 4 voted for the penguins?
   - ☐ $\frac{1}{3}$
   - ☐ $\frac{1}{4}$
   - ☐ $\frac{1}{5}$
   - ☐ $\frac{1}{6}$

4. How many children in question 4 voted for the snakes?
   - ☐ 5
   - ☐ 4
   - ☐ 3
   - ☐ 2

5. Julie read 6 books in January, 13 in February, 21 in March and 24 in April. What was the average number of books she read per month?
   - ☐ 64
   - ☐ 32
   - ☐ 16
   - ☐ 21

6. The average of four numbers is 23. If three of the numbers are 19, 21, and 25, what is the fourth number?
   - ☐ 25
   - ☐ 26
   - ☐ 27
   - ☐ 28

7. Amount of TV watched at the weekend

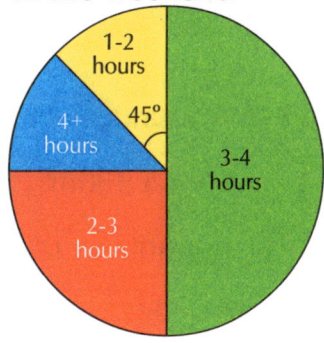

   (pie chart: 1-2 hours, 4+ hours, 45°, 3-4 hours, 2-3 hours)

   If 3 people watch 1–2 hours of TV at the weekend, how many people answered the survey?
   - ☐ 16
   - ☐ 18
   - ☐ 22
   - ☐ 24

Topic 28: Capacity

A. Warm up!

Shade in the specified measurements on each measuring jug.

1. $\frac{1}{2}$ litre
2. $\frac{9}{10}$ litre
3. $\frac{1}{5}$ litre
4. 0·8 litre
5. 0·1 litre
6. $\frac{3}{5}$ litre
7. $\frac{3}{10}$ litre
8. $\frac{7}{10}$ litre

B. Calculate!

1. **Write each of these amounts as litres and millilitres.**

   (a) 2,700ml ___ l ___ ml
   (b) 3,500ml ___ l ___ ml
   (c) 1,050ml ___ l ___ ml
   (d) 2,005ml ___ l ___ ml
   (e) $1\frac{1}{4}$ litres ___ l ___ ml
   (f) $\frac{1}{2}$ litres ___ l ___ ml
   (g) 2·75 litres ___ l ___ ml
   (h) 0·8 litres ___ l ___ ml
   (i) $1\frac{1}{2}$ litres ___ l ___ ml
   (j) $\frac{3}{4}$ litre ___ l ___ ml

2. **Write each of these amounts as litres using the decimal point.**

   (a) 1,500ml ___
   (e) 2l 350ml ___
   (f) 2l 30ml ___
   (g) $2\frac{3}{5}$ l ___

3. **Write each of these amounts as millilitres.**

   (a) 1·45l ___
   (b) 0·95l ___
   (c) 0·7l ___
   (d) $1\frac{3}{10}$ l ___
   (e) $2\frac{4}{5}$ l ___
   (f) 0·75l ___
   (g) $\frac{7}{10}$ l ___
   (h) $2\frac{3}{4}$ l ___
   (i) 0·05l ___
   (j) 0·002l ___

4. **How many millilitres must be added to each of these amounts to make 1 litre?**

   (a) 200ml ___
   (b) 0·3l ___
   (c) $\frac{2}{5}$ l ___
   (d) 0·75l ___
   (e) 0·01l ___
   (f) 0·05l ___
   (g) 0·95l ___
   (h) $\frac{19}{20}$ l ___
   (i) $\frac{99}{100}$ l ___
   (j) $\frac{894}{1000}$ l ___

C. Real life maths

Gráinne is making a tropical smoothie. She is using the following ingredients.

| 200ml of pineapple juice |
| 100ml of mango juice |
| 250ml of banana puree |
| 50ml of yellow melon puree |
| 0·15 litres of coconut milk |
| $\frac{1}{4}$ litre of frozen yoghurt |

1. What quantity of smoothie did Gráinne make in total? _____
2. What fraction of the smoothie was mango juice? _____
3. What fraction of the smoothie was pineapple juice? _____
4. What percentage of the smoothie was banana puree? ___
5. How many millilitres of coconut milk did she use? _____
6. If Gráinne was to make 2 litres of tropical smoothie, what quantity of yellow melon puree would she use? _____

D. Puzzle

Cian is making dinner. He has two containers, one with a capacity of 4 litres and the other with a capacity of 3 litres. He needs to add 1 litre of water to his vegetables. How will he use the containers to get exactly 1 litre of water? _____

E. Word puzzles

1. A can of soft drink holds **330ml**. Half of it is poured into a glass. How many millilitres is that? _____
2. How many millilitres short of **2 litres** is **1$\frac{3}{4}$ litres**? _____
3. If a kettle that holds **500ml** is $\frac{1}{5}$ full. How many millilitres of water are in the kettle? _____
4. What fraction of **5 litres** is **3 litres**? _____
5. **250ml** of water costs **€0·80**. How much is **3$\frac{1}{2}$ litres** of the same water? _____

Test yourself!

1. $\frac{1}{10}$ litre is the same as:
   - ☐ 10ml
   - ☐ 100ml
   - ☐ 1,000ml
   - ☐ 1ml

2. What fraction of 1 litre is 200ml?
   - ☐ $\frac{1}{5}$
   - ☐ $\frac{1}{10}$
   - ☐ $\frac{2}{5}$
   - ☐ $\frac{2}{100}$

3. What is 1·05 litres written as litres and millilitres?
   - ☐ 1l 5ml
   - ☐ 1l 50ml
   - ☐ 1l 500ml
   - ☐ 105ml

4. How much be added to 2·95 litres to make 3 litres?
   - ☐ 5ml
   - ☐ 5 litres
   - ☐ 50ml
   - ☐ 500ml

5. Martin made 5 litres of lemonade for a party. He shared the lemonade equally among 20 glasses. How much lemonade was in each glass?
   - ☐ 20ml
   - ☐ 200ml
   - ☐ 250ml
   - ☐ 500ml

6. What fraction of a 1 litre is 250ml?
   - ☐ $\frac{1}{4}$ litre
   - ☐ $\frac{1}{5}$ litre
   - ☐ 0·3 litre
   - ☐ 800ml

7. $\frac{42}{1000}$ of 1 litre is how many millilitres?
   - ☐ 420ml
   - ☐ 42ml
   - ☐ 4,200ml
   - ☐ 4·2ml

8. A bottle holds 2 litres. Ally puts 0·7l of orange juice into the bottle. How many millilitres more are needed to fill the bottle?
   - ☐ 0·1 litres
   - ☐ 30ml
   - ☐ 300ml
   - ☐ $\frac{1}{4}$ litre

9. Divide 0·75l of water equally into 3 glasses. Each glass gets _____ of water.
   - ☐ 25ml
   - ☐ 250ml
   - ☐ $\frac{3}{4}$ litre
   - ☐ 0·2 litre

10. What percentage of the cylinder is full?
    - ☐ 2%
    - ☐ 20%
    - ☐ 0·2%
    - ☐ 25%

TOPIC 29 Chance

A. Warm up!

Where would you place these events on the probability scale?

Impossible — Unlikely — Even Chance — Likely — Certain

1. You will have an Irish lesson tomorrow. _____
2. You will be President of Ireland when you grow up. _____
3. There are mice living somewhere in your school. _____
4. Someone will die from hunger in the world today. _____
5. You will watch some TV at the weekend. _____

B. In your mathematical opinion

Estimate and then find out what the chance would be of pulling each of these items out of your school bag.

1. A Maths book _____
2. A lunchbox _____
3. A ruler _____
4. An Irish book _____
5. An old sandwich! _____
6. A copy book _____

C. Calculate!

1. (a) What is the chance of rolling a six? _____
   (b) What is the chance of rolling a three? _____
   (c) What is the chance of rolling an even number? _____
   (d) What is the chance of rolling a one, two or three? _____

2. (a) Which colour cube has the most chance of being pulled out of the bag? _____
   (b) Which colour cube has the least chance of being pulled out? _____
   (c) What is the chance of pulling out a blue cube? _____
   (d) What is the chance of pulling out a red cube? _____

D. True or false?

1. There is a greater chance of spinning an even number than an odd number. ☐ true ☐ false
2. The chance of spinning a 9 is 1 in 10. ☐ true ☐ false
3. The chance of spinning a 7 or 8 is 1 in 5. ☐ true ☐ false
4. The chance of spinning a number that is a multiple of 2 is 1 in 3. ☐ true ☐ false
5. There is a 3 in 10 chance of spinning a multiple of 3. ☐ true ☐ false

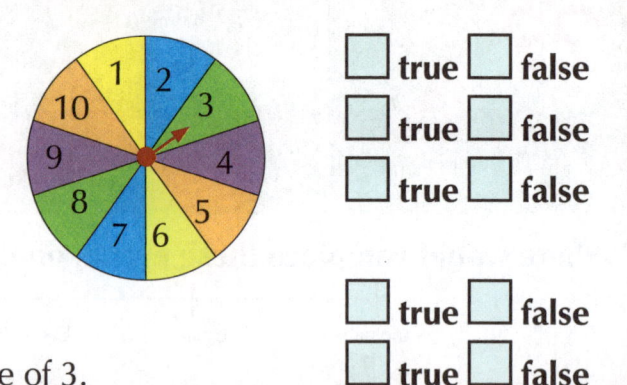

E. Real life maths

1. **Watch the weather forecast each evening. Use the table to record whether or not the weather forecaster was correct.**
   Record the outcome for 30 days. At the end of each 10-day period, calculate the total number of accurate forecasts.

day	1	2	3	4	5	6	7	8	9	10	total	fraction
correct												$\frac{}{10}$
incorrect												$\frac{}{10}$

day	11	12	13	14	15	16	17	18	19	20	total	fraction
correct												$\frac{}{20}$
incorrect												$\frac{}{20}$

day	21	22	23	24	25	26	27	28	29	30	total	fraction
correct												$\frac{}{30}$
incorrect												$\frac{}{30}$

2. How many forecasts were accurate? _____
3. What fraction of forecasts were accurate? _____
4. There is ____ chance in ____ of a weather forecast being correct over a 30-day period.

Test yourself!

1. When you toss a coin, the chance it will land heads up is:

   ☐ 1 in 2   ☐ 1 in 5
   ☐ 1 in 10 ☐ no chance

2. When you toss two coins together, the chance they will both land heads up is:

   ☐ 1 chance in 4
   ☐ 1 chance in 3
   ☐ 2 chances in 5
   ☐ 2 chances in 3

3. There are 3 red cubes, 5 blue cubes and 2 yellow cubes in a bag. Which cube has an even chance of being pulled from the bag?

   ☐ blue   ☐ red
   ☐ yellow ☐ none of them

4. Which cube has a 1 in 5 chance of being pulled from the bag in question 3?

   ☐ blue   ☐ red
   ☐ yellow ☐ none of these

5. When you spin the spinner, there is an even chance of landing on a:

   ☐ train   ☐ bus
   ☐ car   ☐ bicycle

6. When you spin the spinner in question 5 there is a 1 in 4 chance of landing on a:

   ☐ train   ☐ bus
   ☐ car   ☐ bicycle

7. When you spin the spinner in question 5 there is the same chance of a landing on:

   ☐ a bicycle as a bus
   ☐ a bus as a train
   ☐ a car as a bus
   ☐ A train as a bicycle

Planet Maths Activity Book • 5th Class

Let's Look Back

A. Warm up!

Write the value of each of the underlined numbers in (a) numbers and (b) words, e.g. 2,4**8**6 = 400, four hundred.

1. 698   (a)_____ (b)_____
2. 1,143 (a)_____ (b)_____
3. 3,069 (a)_____ (b)_____
4. 5,542 (a)_____ (b)_____
5. 7,863 (a)_____ (b)_____
6. 8,984 (a)_____ (b)_____

B. Calculate!

1. Calculate the answers.

   (a) 18 + 9 + 1,186 = ___
   (b) 3,294 − 1,169 = ___
   (c) 281 + 8,329 + 9 = ___
   (d) 1,086 − 247 = ___
   (e) 5,521 − 86 = ___
   (f) (498 + 6,329) − 94 = ___

2. Write these fractions in decimal form.

   (a) $\frac{1}{10}$ = ___
   (b) $\frac{3}{10}$ = ___
   (c) $\frac{7}{10}$ = ___
   (d) $\frac{19}{10}$ = ___
   (e) $\frac{11}{100}$ = ___
   (f) $2\frac{79}{100}$ = ___

C. Time

1. A train leaves Heuston Station in Dublin for Westport at the following times. If the journey takes 3 hours 35 minutes, write the time when each train reaches Westport.

Start time:	8:24	11:35	2:05	4:10	5:56
arrival time					

2. Each clock shows a time that is 55 minutes fast. Write the correct time in digit form.

   (a) _____ (b) _____ (c) _____ (d) _____ (e) _____

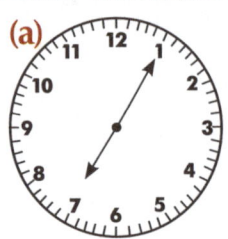

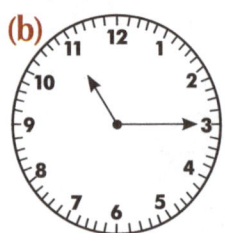

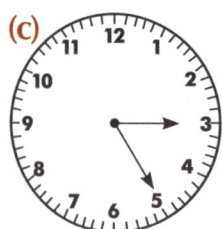

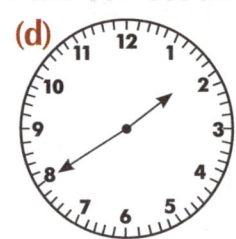

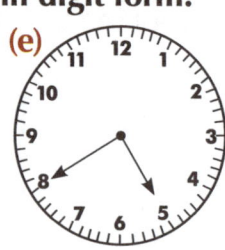

B. Calculate!

Calculate the answers.

1. (a) 29 × 65 = ___   (b) $\frac{248}{8}$ = ___   (c) 206 × 17 = ___
   (d) $\frac{206}{5}$ = ___ R ___   (e) $\frac{119}{8}$ = ___ R ___

2. (a) 336 ÷ 9 = ___ R ___   (b) 4·89 × 7 = ___   (c) 7·83 ÷ 3 = ___
   (d) 9·48 ÷ 6 = ___   (e) $6\frac{19}{100}$ × 8 = ___

E. Shapes

Name each of these 2D shapes.

1.    2. 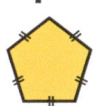   3. 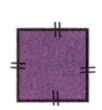   4.

5. 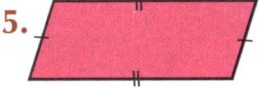   6.    7.    8.

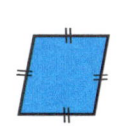

F. Calculate!

1. **Calculate the answers.**

   (a) $\frac{1}{2}$ of 16 = ___   (b) $\frac{3}{8}$ of 32 = ___   (c) $\frac{3}{5}$ of 35 = ___   (d) $\frac{2}{3}$ of 63 = ___
   (e) 0·1 of 10 = ___   (f) 0·3 of 50 = ___   (g) 0·5 of 24 = ___   (h) 0·8 of 25 = ___

2. **Fill in the equivalent fractions.**

   (a) $\frac{}{2} = \frac{2}{4}$ (b) $\frac{1}{3} = \frac{3}{}$
   (c) $\frac{}{4} = \frac{9}{12}$ (d) $\frac{1}{} = \frac{2}{10}$
   (e) $\frac{2}{} = \frac{4}{6}$ (f) $\frac{}{5} = \frac{4}{10}$
   (g) $\frac{5}{6} = \frac{}{12}$ (h) $\frac{4}{} = \frac{8}{10}$

Test yourself!

1. $3\frac{9}{10}$ as an improper fraction is:
   - ☐ $\frac{30}{10}$
   - ☐ $3\frac{10}{9}$
   - ☐ $3\frac{9}{10}$
   - ☐ $3\frac{1}{10}$

2. $1\frac{4}{5} + 2\frac{7}{10} =$ ___
   - ☐ $3\frac{47}{15}$
   - ☐ $3\frac{11}{15}$
   - ☐ $3\frac{15}{10}$
   - ☐ $4\frac{1}{2}$

3. $3\frac{1}{6} - 2\frac{2}{3} =$ ___
   - ☐ $\frac{1}{2}$
   - ☐ $1\frac{1}{3}$
   - ☐ $\frac{3}{9}$
   - ☐ $\frac{1}{3}$

4. $\frac{7}{8} \times 9 =$ ___
   - ☐ $\frac{79}{89}$
   - ☐ $\frac{63}{81}$
   - ☐ $7\frac{7}{8}$
   - ☐ $\frac{7}{72}$

5. What types of angles are these?
   - ☐ a = acute, b = reflex
   - ☐ a = reflex, b = acute
   - ☐ a = obtuse, b = acute
   - ☐ a = full rotation, b = obtuse

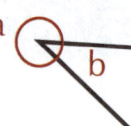

6. The value of the underlined digit in the number 245·683 is:
   - ☐ 3 thousands
   - ☐ 3 hundredths
   - ☐ 3 tenths
   - ☐ 3 thousandths

7. $\frac{53}{1000}$ written as a decimal is:
   - ☐ 0·53
   - ☐ 0·053
   - ☐ 0·0053
   - ☐ 5·03

8. The first four multiples of 3 are:
   - ☐ 3, 6, 9, 12
   - ☐ 6, 9, 12, 15
   - ☐ 1, 3, 6, 9
   - ☐ 1, 2, 3, 4

9. The product of the pairs of factors 12 and 4 is:
   - ☐ 48
   - ☐ 16
   - ☐ 8
   - ☐ 46

10. The prime numbers between 10 and 20 are:
    - ☐ 11, 15, 17, 19
    - ☐ 11, 13, 15, 17, 19
    - ☐ 11, 13, 17, 19
    - ☐ 12, 14, 15, 18

Test yourself!

11. A square with an area of 81m² has a perimeter of:

☐ 9m ☐ 18m
☐ 27m ☐ 36m

12. 79·25 ÷ 25 = ___

☐ 3·17 ☐ 31·70
☐ 0·317 ☐ 317

13. 3·08 ÷ 44 = ___

☐ 7   ☐ 0·7
☐ 0·07 ☐ 0·007

14. In 24-hour clock format, twenty to ten at night is:

☐ 22:40 ☐ 9:40 pm
☐ 09:40 ☐ 21:40

15. 2 hours 52 minutes before 17:30 is:

☐ 14:78 ☐ 14:38
☐ 14:08 ☐ 15:38

16. 40% written as a decimal is:

☐ 2/5 ☐ 0·4
☐ 0·04 ☐ 4·0

17. Gillian scored 4 out of 5 in a test. What was her score as a percentage?

_____

☐ 50% ☐ 40%
☐ 45% ☐ 80%

18. Increase €12 by 50%.

☐ €62 ☐ €6
☐ €18 ☐ €24

19. Reduce €200 by 20%.

☐ €40 ☐ €160
☐ €180 ☐ €220

20. What is the chance of pulling out a red marble from a bag with 6 red marbles, 3 blue marbles, 2 yellow marbles and 1 blue marble?

☐ even   ☐ 1 in 6
☐ 5 in 12 ☐ 12 in 6

rough work

rough work

ROUGH WORK